DEVON

FOLK TALES FOR CHILDREN

DEVON

FOLK TALES FOR CHILDREN

LEONIE JANE-GREY

First published 2019

Reprinted 2020

The History Press
The Mill, Brimscombe Port
Stroud, Gloucestershire, GL5 2QG
www.thehistorypress.co.uk

British Library Cataloguing in Publication Data.
A catalogue record for this book is available from the British Library.

ISBN 978 0 7509 8444 7

Typesetting and origination by The History Press
Printed and bound in Great Britain by TJ Books Ltd.

CONTENTS

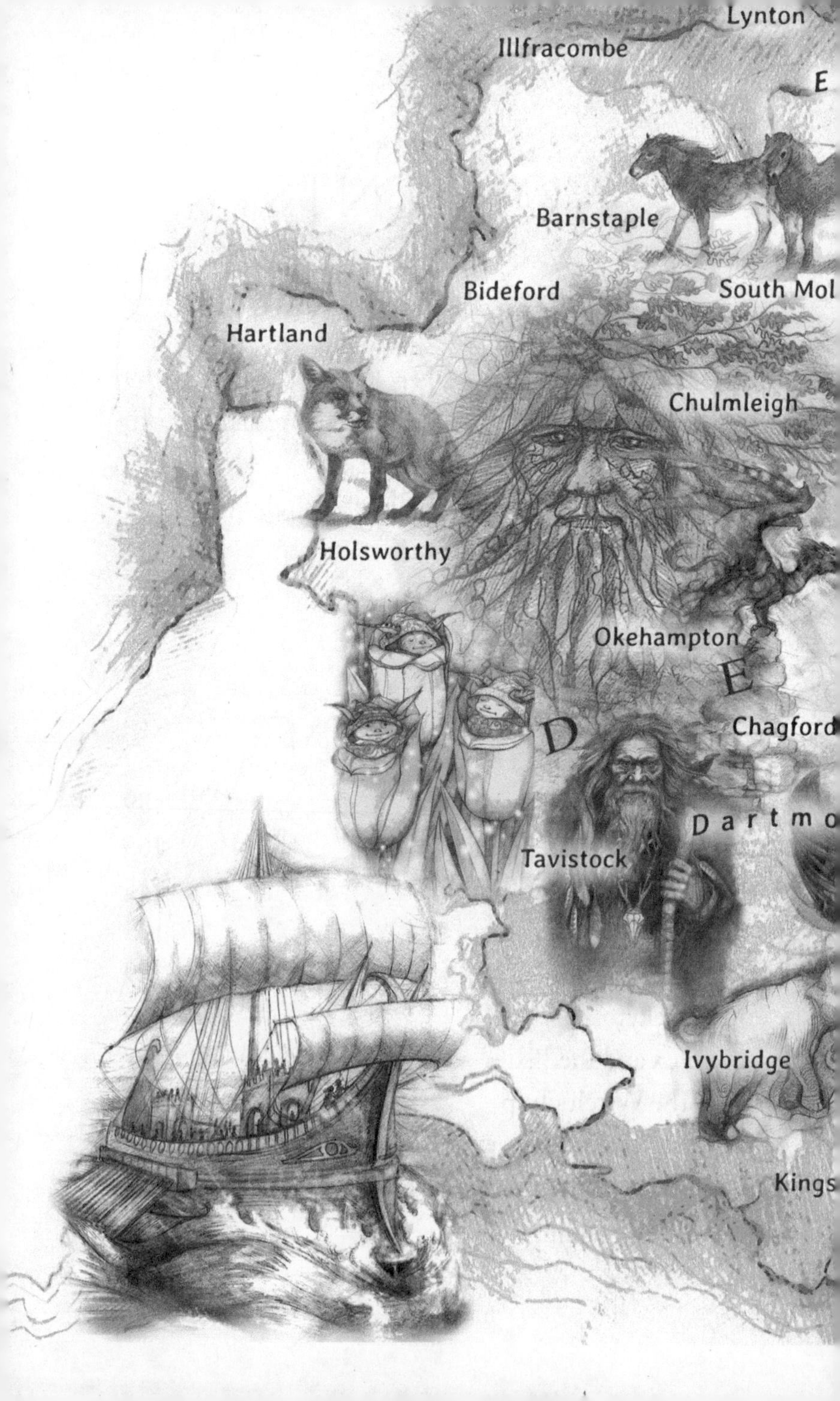
Lynton
Illfracombe
Barnstaple
Bideford
South Mol
Hartland
Chulmleigh
Holsworthy
Okehampton
Chagford
Dartmo
Tavistock
Ivybridge
Kings

o r
Tiverton
Cullompton
Blackdown Hills
Crediton
O N
Exeter
Sidmouth
Exmouth
Torquay

FOREWORD

When I was a little girl, I used to lie down daily at the foot of a local oak tree. Mighty, old and welcoming, it was the theatre of my first storytellings. Here I studied the clouds for messages and listened to the birds' secrets. I gathered acorn cups and raindrops and prepared invisible feasts for the little folk that lived amongst its roots. Every day after school, this sacred place sprang to life before my eyes; the site of daily battles, dramas and mysteries.

So entranced was I by this special place, that no well-meaning adult would have been able to convince me my fairy imaginings were not real. Of course, I wasn't the first child to do this and shall certainly not be the last.

This is a scene that has been playing out beneath the leafy trees of Britain forever.

I suppose my question is: why do we take to the wonders of story so young and so passionately? I suspect the answer is that folklore is in our blood, that it lives in the very marrow of our bones. In the way that swallows feel the call of the African plains or wolves howl in unison, human beings have a need to share stories. Long may it continue.

However, amidst the clamour and glamour of the digital age, the old stories are at risk of being lost. We are tremendously fortunate that Devon has some of the last truly wild places in England and a storytelling tradition to match. In this fascinating and beautifully illustrated collection, Leonie Jane-Grey turns the volume back up on the old songs, bright and loud.

Ask yourself: do you know why the South Devon soil is so red? Have you ever seen a mysterious dark creature lurking in the tangled river weed? Has the shadow of a silver hare racing across a moonlit hill ever caught your eye? Have you ever heard a fairy prince speak with a voice of a skylark?

You haven't? Well then, I would suggest it's high time you changed that. Lie down, pick up this book and lose yourself in the timeless rhythm and wonder of story.

Claire Barker
Children's author

1

DEVON

Land of the Deep Valley Dwellers

Long ago, so long ago it was a time before time, a small patch of ground nestled within the palm of the largest supercontinent the Earth has ever known – it was the small piece of Earth which was to become Devon. Over eons, the continents slid and groaned and heaved apart. Those already-ancient rocks that were to form Devon continued on their slow journey. Eventually, perhaps for a brief flicker in deep time, the ever-changing land would be divided up by humans into the world map we know today.

The land on which we stand is ancient. Devon hums with a thousand primordial songs. If we put our ear to the ground, down really low, perhaps we will hear stories of ice ages and forests, tundra and cave lions, deep in the black and red soil. Imagine the first amphibians that crawled out from the sea, their web-toes slapping over slick mud. The ooze over which they slithered has been squeezed and shaped by the great movements of the Earth to become shale and mudstone beneath our own bare feet. The rocks along the Devon coastlines contain the fossilized memories of waters once teeming with ancient sea life. Sheltering hillside hollows and Devon caves remember the songs of great lizards, mammoth, hippo, blackbird, mole, dragonfly, beetle and bee.

The Devon hills ring with the echoes of blows from flint axes made by our ancestors. Wild humans followed bands of wild horses over the land-bridge called Doggerland, when the seas were still lower than they

are today and Britain had not yet become an island. Perhaps when we rest in our gardens we may sense their sharp stories of dark caves, glowing fire, fierce hunting, and how they imagined the world must have been created.

Wave after wave of people have arrived to this green island. Sometimes people arrived here peacefully, but often with violent battle. Our story-soaked fields shudder with the sounds of clashing Viking, Saxon and Roman swords.

Today, Buzzard throws a broad sickle shape against the clouds as he soars high over the land. As he sweeps by catch hold of his tail feathers. Buzzard is powerful enough to carry us all – his wings are broad enough, beaten strong by storms, bronzed by the sun and burnished by the wind, to lift us high over the land. From here we can see hedgerows, fields, farms, villages and towns rolling beneath us. Many rivers thread their way through the deep valleys, and the land is edged along two sides with the wild and sparkling sea. There are many white horses leaping in the waves along these ancient Jurassic coastlines.

Down on the ground, in some distant time, our ancestors are drumming. We gather around their ancient fire. Pixies are dancing in the dusk half-light – the Devon dimpsey time. A giant takes measured strides towards the cliff edge of his fate, and the light of the moon shines in the eyes of a silvered hare witch.

Fox is here to guide us. She is a sharp-eyed hunter with a keen ear for a good story. Her thick coat shows white, red and black against moss green ground. Fox can see far down the road and smell a discarded chicken bone from a whole score mile away. It is time to follow her neat tracks over bog, tor, clitter, riverbank, and through the streets of small towns. The stories are waiting, weaving silvered pathways above and below and over the land. As we gaze out from our own familiar homes, our schools, our workplaces, a vision emerges. We are in an earlier time. Raven is calling.

Turn your coat inside-out lest the pixies lead you astray. May a magpie jump in your path as you travel, to bring you luck.

2

THE FALL OF A GIANT: BRUTUS OF TROY

Goddess kissed and dream driven,
Son of Troy, King of Britain.
Here you stand and here you rest,
Exiled to rule in old Totnes.
Once, a long time ago …

Goddess Diana gazed down upon the blue and green jewel that was the earth. Far below, a wooden ship sailed over a vast ocean. The goddess came close, her breath the sea breeze,

her gossamer tresses shrouding the ship in sea mists, to see what human adventure was unfolding. Brutus of Troy, exiled from Italy after his own stray hunting arrow had killed his father, had set out over the seas, trusting his fate to the winds and the gods. Diana watched him and his Trojan men over weeks and months until they came upon a small deserted island. The adventurers landed ashore desperate to find clean water and food, and keen to explore the island's golden beaches, sun-warmed coves and shaded forest.

Brutus made his way into the interior of the island, seeking deer in the deepest part of the forest, when he happened upon the ruins of an ancient building. Crumbling stone walls enclosed an ancient sanctuary. An exquisite white statue of a goddess stood by the remains of an altar. Brutus thought it wise to bring gifts and make offerings to this beautiful goddess, so she might bless their journey. He returned to the ship and chose a pure white deer from amongst those which had been hunted by his men that day.

His took the heart, the skin, and a goblet of dark red blood. He carried his rich offerings to the temple, laid out the white deer hide on the ground and carefully placed the heart and the goblet upon the altar. Brutus lay down upon the hide and eventually slipped into a deep and dreamless sleep. As dawn broke softly, Goddess Diana came to him.

Diana gave Brutus a dream – the shimmering image of a great dragon-green island, rich with life, running with pure, clean rivers – the promise of a new home. As dawn broke Brutus awoke, dazed and enchanted by his vision. A fire for adventure burned in his heart anew. Swiftly he returned to his men and his ship. Without delay, they set sail over the wide curve of the ocean. Keen, unfailing winds pushed them through swell and rain, the ship moved swiftly, even on still days, until Brutus saw the thin green line of new land ahead. As they approached he saw wild beaches and magnificent hills rising before them. Brutus was certain this was the land of his vision – promised to him by Diana, the goddess of his dreams.

GOEMAGOG

Tree Stride, Boulder Bones,
Chew the world with teeth of stones.
Raven's Rock, your heart so hale,
Still Diana's dream prevails.

Goemagog cut a mighty figure. A behemoth. A giant. Great cloths woven from roots, reeds and sinew covered his ox frame. His shirt had been sewn with a lion-bone needle, and fastened at the breast with an antler pin. A wealth of fox, red deer and bear skins, skulls and teeth had become his cloak. Ravens had given glossy feathers to adorn the tangle of his hair. His grief-twisted state betrayed the rough beauty of his looks – flint eyes, crag brow, cliff jaw. Cast-iron rage boiled in the pot of his gut.

Goemagog had watched a proud wooden ship make its way slowly up into the great mouth of the River Dart. Many men had climbed out and set about taking stones, wood, water, fish, birds, deer. They spoke a language from far away, and carried sharp weapons which shone wickedly in the sun. The leader of the vessel and his followers had lit fires, made noisy celebrations long into dark nights.

The giant families, a rugged bunch of towering earth-movers and cave-dwellers, retreated fearfully to Dartmoor. Amongst them was Goemagog, their strongest and most magnificent champion. After many nights of watching with reddened eyes and gritted teeth, Goemagog and a ragged group of his kindred had moved off the hill. They crashed into a Trojan party intent on ending the ransacking of their treasured hills and valleys. But the educated invaders were trained fighters, quick and sharp in skill and wit. By the night's hard finish, they had taken the giants down, all but one – Goemagog. He had fought with the strength of a mountain. Now he was held captive, a mighty land-master brought down low, feet and hands tied with rough rope, his brothers gone.

CAPTAIN CORINEUS

Hunter thief, slayer of hoards,
Axe wielding warrior, murderous sport.

Corineus eyed the dark, bearded heap of the captive giant.

'Let me fight him, Brutus,' he said, savagely.

'Corineus, you are truly mighty, and a great warrior,' replied Brutus, 'but he's one heck of a beast to take down on your own!'

'Size is no matter; my skill will prevail!' Corineus boasted. He threw his shoulders back and squared up to where Goemagog sat, tied in ropes on the floor. The giant leaned heavily over like a broken tree. Inside, a storm raged.

'He has no sword, no fast weapon to match yours – he has only that great staff, a stone axe, a bear's claw. Hardly fair.'

'No weapons then – I'll wrestle him! Everyone will see that my skill is superior to his size. When I win, reward me with all of the lands to the west of here – I will rid the hills of these overgrown cave-cattle and govern the region for you. Do me the honour of allowing me to name the place after myself – 'Cornwall!'

Brutus laughed – he knew his ferocious and ambitious Captain Corineus well.

'Very well. You will fight him in the morning. We'll see how strong you are: perhaps you will win your patch, your "Cornwall". It is only a small part of my great island after all, which will be named "Britain" after me!'

THE FIGHT

Goemagog watched the Trojan soldiers. They formed neat lines around a space which had been cleared for the fight, close to the cliff-edge of the glittering coastline. He was to wrestle the one who strode amongst them like a cockerel in a new hen pen. A confident fellow considering he was so small. A few of the giants had come too. They stood a little way back and raised their great arms in salute to Goemagog, their own brave warrior, their only champion. This was their home, the very earth of their birth, their beloved clifftops – not far from a place which would one day be known as Plymouth Hoe.

The time had come. The two circled each other. Corineus became quiet, focused on the job. He was no fool when it came to war. And he was fast. He got in quick and low, seeking to unbalance the great weight of the towering giant, trip him up, tip him over. Goemagog, a force of nature, let out a frightening roar. He grabbed Corineus by the scruff and tried smash him with his fist. Corineus twisted away. The giant was shockingly strong, but Corineus knew the ways in which he was weak. The Trojan was trained in clever technique.

Again Corineus ran in, prodding and then dodging, dancing ever out of reach again and again until the giant's rage blew like a hurricane. Dust was stamped and kicked into dry air, their backs grew sweaty. The fight edged ever closer to the clifftops.

Corineus began to tire, almost outlasted by the lean, hill-roving native. At last Goemagog grabbed the man and hugged him with his two huge arms. They circled the Trojan's ribs and tightened – slow and sure the way oak roots grow, Goemagog squeezed ... **CRACK!** one rib, **CRACK!** two ribs, **CRACK!** three ribs broken. Captain Corineus gasped for air but kept his head. He pushed hard and low against the massive frame of the giant, rolling his shoulder the way he knew how. Goemagog furiously tried to get his weight below the man, lever him up, smash him down, end the match. But then a fatal mistake – in his anger he lost his balance. Skilled Corineus caught the momentum, and with all his might he rolled the great giant over his back, staggered a few steps further and just managed to slip from Goemagog's grip as the giant turned clear over, falling into air, over the cliff edge.

Goemagog, brave giant-heart, fell. As he fell he took leave of this world and found his way into the next. To honour his passing and remember him well, the cliff and the earth around, and for a time even the sea below, turned rich, iron-rust red.

Earth and sea, his soul to keep,
Remember him well, Goemagog's Leap.

3

OLD GRANDMOTHER SILVER, HARE WITCH

Once, a young girl lived with her parents in a tiny cottage not far from Tavistock. She had grown up amongst the wind-blown bracken and broom which grew over Dartmoor – a girl with a far-away look in her eyes. Often, at the end of the day, she would slip out from beneath the hard shine of the lamplight within their little home and head into the soft twilight of the moors. Then she would run barefoot along narrow sheep tracks towards the moonlight, the sting of rain on her face and hair streaming in the wind.

One moon-bright night, when she was perhaps still only just eight years old, she ran so fast towards the moon her heart hammered in her chest, the wind tore the breath from her body ... and then ... and then she changed! She became a hare – a bright, moonshine-eyed moorland hare! Oh, how she ran then, on four strong legs, wild with joy.

A Hare's joy bounding,
Silvered tracks winding.
Moonshine magic,
Of a wild soul unbinding.

Many years had gone by. The young girl was grown old, so old she was known only as Old Grandmother Silver – since the nights of running over the moors under the moonlight had made her hair white and streaked with silvered light. The wind had blown deep lines of laughter into her face. She was as old as those Dartmoor hills, so her grandson Robin thought. Now he lived with her in just the same tiny cottage, which leaned against the slope of the moor near Tavistock. She was the only one in the world he had to care for him.

They had very little money, barely enough for a little this and a little that. Clothes were patched and mended. They were lucky if they happened to find a fallen silver sixpence in a street gutter to spend at Tavistock market. Times grew very tough for Robin and his grandmother – they had to use their wits to survive. Then, one cold, grey morning Old Grandmother Silver looked into Robin's eyes and took his hands in hers.

'Grandson, we must have something to eat,' she said firmly. 'There is something I will tell you, but know this – if I do you must keep my secret in the deepest part of your heart. If anyone else were to know, it will be bad for me.'

'I can keep your secret Grandmother,' Robbin said, nodding his head.

'Listen now. When I was a girl, not much younger than you, the moors called to me so strongly that I would slip out from the house and run barefoot into the night. When I ran as fast as I could I changed. I don't know how, or why, but I became a wild hare. Eventually I could do this even in the daytime. I practiced until I could become a hare and change back into me again just as I wanted.'

Robin stared hard at Old Grandmother Silver. He knew how affected she was by the wildness of the moors. Somewhere, in a deep place in his soul where there are no words, he understood.

'You must never tell anyone Robin. People will say I am a witch; it will be very dangerous for me.'

'I never will. It's our secret now,' said Robin simply. 'But how will this help us find something to eat?'

'Robin, I want you to go visit the Squire. He's a miserable old boot but he does love his hunting. Tell him you've seen a fine hare by the hedge in his Longacre field – maybe he'll give you a sixpence for saying so.'

'And you will be the fine hare waiting for him? But Grandmother, what if his dogs catch you?' Robin asked, his eyes wide with alarm.

'Don't be afraid for me Robin. I may be very old, but when I am a hare I can still run as fast as the wind can blow.'

Robin felt worried but he set off to find the Squire as Old Grandmother Silver had asked him to. He found him at his stable yard, where he was watching his men work.

'What do you want lad?' demanded the Squire as Robin approached. The Squire had a sour feel about him.

'Sir, I came to tell you I have seen a fine hare by the hedge in your Longacre field – I know you love to hunt.'

'Ah! Good, a fine hare!' The Squire leaped to his feet. 'Here's a silver sixpence for your trouble young man. Be off home now.' Robin took the money tightly in his fist and scurried away across the cobbled yard. He could hear the Squire shouting orders behind him: 'Saddle the horses! Bring the dogs!'

Robin ran as fast as he could over the Squire's land towards Longacre. There he saw a large brown hare standing up on her long hind legs for all to see. Her coat was rich and tawny, her ears edged in silver. Three men, three horses and ten dogs thundered by, spattering Robin with wet turf. The hare leaped away onto the moors with a flick of her broad hind feet. Robin stopped in his tracks. He could only stare helplessly as the men, horses, dogs and hare all disappeared over the hill.

Robin ran all the way home. There he found Old Grandmother Silver in the cottage, her hair hanging in knotted strands, her legs muddied and scratched. She held out a shaking hand towards the boy.

'Did you get the sixpence?' she asked, smiling. Robbin dropped the silver sixpence into her palm.

Several times Robin went to the Squire with his news of a large brown hare and each time the Squire gave Robin a silver sixpence for his trouble. But after a time, the Squire became suspicious – how was it that the same boy always knew the whereabouts of the same large hare? Each time the Squire set out hunting he somehow lost the hare in a muddy scramble over the moors. A pattern was emerging … and then one day the Squire noticed an old woman hurrying away down the lane, just where the hare had slipped away. Strange how her legs were muddied, her skirt hem torn. The Squire suspected trickery.

The next time the Squire saw Robin he was ready. The horses were already saddled and the dogs waiting.

'Where is the hare?' the Squire demanded.

'By the Old Oak Tree,' said Robin pale with fright.

The Squire threw Robin a sixpence and the hunt was away from the yard like fury. A field away the hare saw them coming and fled for her life. After miles of zig-zagging over the moors she scrambled into a tangled patch of thicket, the hounds snapping at her heels and the huntsmen right behind. The men drove their horses headlong in after her but somehow, again, she vanished. Without pause the Squire pushed his horse out from the mess of branches and briar towards a nearby lane. He saw only a bent over, silver haired old woman shambling away as fast as she could. He pulled up sharply stared. The old woman's legs were covered in bramble scratches and she was breathing hard, as though she had been running. Was there some witchcraft at work here?

The Squire rode his exhausted, mud-spattered horse directly to the Parson's house. The Parson knew Robin, and knew where he lived with Old Grandmother Silver, and together they made a plan.

'Watch the boy closely. When he comes give him one last sixpence, then you know what to do,' said the Parson, his mouth set in a cruel, determined line.

Robin had found Old Grandmother Silver at home, scratched and bruised and badly shaken.

'Grandmother, this is too dangerous! We must stop!' he cried.

'Robin, you must go to the Squire one last time. Just one more sixpence or we will starve this winter! Then no more, I promise.'

Robin shook his head sadly. He was sure his grandmother would be caught. Reluctantly

Robin made his way to the Squire's house as he was asked. This time the Squire watched him coming.

'Where is the hare?' he demanded, his movements savage as he mounted his already prepared horse.

'By the pond in your Big Field,' said Robin, his face pale and his hands shaking as he picked up the silver coin the Squire had tossed on the floor.

The hounds were ready, the best horses were ready, the men already in the saddle. Even the Parson was there on his big brown mare. They let loose the dogs.

'Run Grandmother, RUN!' Robin screamed.

The hunt was away, scattering mud and grit. The hare fled for her life. The dogs were fast, catching at her heals – teeth bared like they were driven by the Wild Huntsman himself, their tongues hanging out and red-rimmed eyes blazing. They were too close for Old Grandmother Silver to change into a woman without being caught. Instead she bolted for home but the huntsmen saw her go. They galloped after her towards the tiny house. The hare fled before them and jammed herself straight in through a small hole in the cottage door.

The Squire rode right up to the house and threw himself down from his horse. He battered the little front door with his whip, dogs crowding round baying furiously all the while. The Parson pushed his way to the front.

'Stand back! I will deal with this witchcraft!' he yelled, and rammed the door with his shoulder. It gave in easily, splintering wood across the small kitchen inside. Robin arrived at the scene, his breaths shuddering in his chest from running all the way home, and watched helplessly as the Parson, several dogs, the Squire and even the Squire's horse all pushed their way into the cottage.

There was no hare to be seen. Up the stairs the Parson and Squire and half the dogs crashed and clattered. There on the little wooden bed, shaking and sobbing and panting hard for breath, lay the old woman.

'Look! A dog bite on her leg!' shouted the Squire.

'Let the dogs have her – they will smell if she is a changing woman, a hare witch!' spat the Parson.

'No! No! No! Not the dogs!' cried Old Grandmother Silver. 'I'll tell you everything – but please spare an old woman and a little boy with no one else in the world to care for him!'

Cruel though they were, the men pulled the dogs back and looked at Robin.

'True enough old woman.' growled the Squire. He had no desire to have a starving orphan boy on his hands. 'I will spare you this once. But if you ever use witchcraft to deceive me again it will be the end of you!'

'Never! Never again!' sobbed Old Grandmother Silver.

After a terrible while of questioning, threats, and the cottage being searched, the men and dogs and horses left. The garden was a trampled mess, the door shattered, and Old Grandmother Silver scratched, bitten and shaken. But all had become quiet in the little house. Robin, his face pale, still smeared with mud and streaked with tears, held out his fist towards Old Grandmother Silver. He slowly uncurled his tightly gripped fingers. A silver sixpence shone in the palm of his hand.

'Aye, we'll have a little loaf of warm bread for our supper tonight,' Grandmother Silver said, and smiled. She took the little coin gently from Robin. 'But I think I'd best leave it a little while before I run again.'

4

THE TULIP PIXIES

Some long while back, an old woman lived alone, quietly in her cottage. She kept her home beautifully, but her pride and joy was her small garden. It was loved and tended well, and yet she allowed it to remain perfectly wild enough so that many small creatures made their home there. Flowers bloomed and nodded in the breeze – roses, geranium, precious old forget-me-nots and marigolds for the bees, and ivy grew in fabulous tangles over the hip-high wall. If you went there you might feel like you had wandered into some small, magical kingdom.

Fields stretched away from two sides of the old woman's house. Sometimes green rings appeared in the grass near the house, as though some wild animals had gathered in a circle and worked spells beneath the stars. Some said the markings were made by elves who played at catching hold of a Dartmoor colt by the tail and dancing him round and round until he drew a circle in the grass with his hard little feet.

The old woman smiled at these stories. The whisperings of the roe deer and the night ceremonies of badger, fox and crow were not new to her. And she had seen the ragged little Dartmoor ponies dancing for joy in the fields at dawn, but she had her own thoughts about those circles in the grass.

During the day the old woman tended her garden, whispering to the flowers as she went. Of them all, her tulips stole the show. Strong and tall, they gave her dazzling flowers in radiant orange, red, and yellow. These she tended with extra care. She touched the blossoms rarely, only if she really had to and with the gentlest movements. Later, as the twilight drew down over Dartmoor, the old woman would sit in her chair by the open kitchen window, watch and listen.

The softest sounds drifted across the garden, caressing the flowers, slipping into the kitchen – a strange, musical sound, as though the flowers were humming of their blossoming, or for all the world as though the birds were singing a lullaby. Then she saw the smallest movements amongst the ivy and the oxeye daisies. Small creatures were climbing over the garden wall and into the flowerbeds – pixies!

The pixies loved the gentle old woman. They loved how she tended the garden and the flowers. They saw how she took care not to tread on small creatures – the snails and beetles, spiders and butterflies. So on certain nights they came, perhaps when the wind blew in just the right direction and all of the stars were in just the right places. The pixies brought their tiny babies and placed each one inside a tulip flower. They curled and tucked the sweet-smelling petals round them, rocked the flowers gently and sang their lullabies.

The old woman watched, spellbound, as these little wild creatures looked over to her and showed her their precious children. When all the tiny babies were fast asleep the grown-up pixies would quietly slip away into the field to dance – a whirling, twirling circle dance. At dawn, while the old woman dozed in her chair, the pixies would gather up their young ones from the tulip flowers

and melt away into the moorland dawn – leaving only green rings in the grass as a sign of their passing.

With each night visit the old woman's tulips grew ever more radiant. The blooms lasted far longer than any other, their scent sweeter than roses, so blessed were they by the songs of the pixies.

Year on year the old woman tended her garden. Always the tulips grew strong and tall, and blossomed radiantly. Always there were marigolds for the bees, and some nettles, so loved by the butterflies, were allowed to flower and seed. So it was for a long time, but no one can live forever, and try as she might it came time for the old woman to walk from this world into the next, and so she died. The cottage was renovated and after a short time, the old place was sold.

The new people had no time for quaint stories about pixies. They knew nothing of a magical kingdom in the garden. They threw out the oxeyes, the roses, and the marigolds. They dug over the soil. They cared only for what they could take – apples and pears from the trees, raspberries and blackcurrants from the bushes.

An old man from down the lane looked on one day. He had known the old woman for a long time.

'You shouldn't take so much from the garden and give nothing in return. It will lead to trouble for you – the pixies will feel robbed!' he said.

'What silly nonsense,' the new people said. A day later they threw out the tulips and dug over the soil. Room for onions.

The next time the old man walked by he stopped and stared at the raw empty earth where the tulips had stood.

'The old woman who lived here loved those tulips. She was my friend,' he said, with a tear in his eye.

'Life moves on. We want to grow vegetables,' the new people replied. They thought the old man should mind his own business. But nothing would ever grow in the soil where the old woman's tulips had been. Not an onion, not a carrot, not a cabbage, not a bean. The once magical garden became a sad and silent place. The birds moved away, the bees were long gone.

A few miles away the old woman's grave lay nestled in the ground in an old churchyard. No one could ever explain how it happened, but after a time forget-me-nots began to grow there. Soon after that grew the marigolds – bees came to visit and hum sweetly. Next oxeye daisies sprang up, wild dog-rose began to grow and blossom by the grave-yard wall nearby, and ivy began to climb in a fantastic tangle over the hip-high gravestone. And then the tulips came, tall and strong, with flowers in radiant orange, red, and yellow. And who can say ... perhaps if the breeze blew in just the right way and the stars happened to be in just the right place, wild pixies climbed the graveyard wall bringing a satchel full of seeds, an acorn-cup of honey, a silken spider-web blessing. They may even have tucked their tiny babies to sleep in the tulip flowers, which rocked and swayed gently to a strange music – as though the flowers were humming, and the birds were singing the sweetest lullaby.

Pixie magic, this dance they know,
Nature sees your garden grow.
Truth will out and beauty shine,
Nature sees this heart of mine.

5

OLD CROCKERN DREAMING

An Original Introduction to 'A Man from Manchester'

by Leonie Jane-Grey

In a time before time began, Old Grandfather Crockern was dreaming the moor.

He was dreaming the living rocks of the moor – the beloved bold heap of his own Crockern Tor, great boulders, worn river stones, grit. The rocks themselves dreamed of deep time, slow time. They dreamed of the Earth bubbling and spitting red lava, the flowing and splitting of hard ice, being carried by glaciers and then left heaped and scattered over the landscape as though they were leaves fallen and blown from a tree.

They dreamed of the sun warming them as they lay on the surface of the Earth, and of being river-tumbled, smoothed, polished, ground down to gravel. Old Crockern saw that the rocks and the stones served life, because on them rested everything else.

Old Grandfather Crockern dreamed the clean, living waters of the moor – the beloved streams creeping out from the dark earth. The waters themselves dreamed of leaping, rolling, and splashing. They dreamed of digging and carving channels through wet mud, and of joyful silver fish playing. They dreamed of still pools, sunlight sparkles, insects sipping from droplets, ponds, lakes, rain and sleet. They dreamed of flowing out into the sea, meeting and mixing with salt, depth, and vastness … Old Crockern saw that the clean waters of the moor served life, because without clean water nothing can live.

Old Grandfather Crockern dreamed the living soils of the moor – the beloved dark and warm blanket which covers the Earth. The soils themselves dreamed of a trillion microscopic forms brewing and bubbling with rich chemistry. They dreamed of heaps of leaves, of being turned and churned by earthworms and beetles, and tiny seeds breaking open and putting out new brave roots. They dreamed of old trees reaching down deep, and many kinds of buried treasure. Old Crockern saw that the clean soils of the moor served life, because without clean soils nothing can grow.

Old Grandfather Crockern dreamed the moors … he dreamed the grasses, the gorse, the bracken and the hawthorn trees. He dreamed damsel flies and horseflies, the mice, the sparrows, the ravens and the buzzards. He dreamed the black fox, and Dewer's difficult red-eyed Whisht dogs and their galloping hunt. He dreamed badgers, and ponies, and cows and he dreamed the sheep. He dreamed the hills, the slopes, the deep valleys, and his beloved stacks of granite. He dreamed the great frowning clouds and driving rain, the lofty stands of evergreens, the twisted oaks and the wise men of Whistman's Woods. He dreamed of the chattering, laughing, arguing people who had gathered on the rocks of Crockern Tor to debate their business. He dreamed the big, wide sky. And he smiled, because he loved them all. So it was.

Until, that is, Old Grandfather Crockern saw down the road a stranger travelling towards his beloved moor – a man from Manchester.

6

THE MAN FROM MANCHESTER

A wealthy businessman travelled from his home town in the North of England to Devon. During his stay he thought that some of the poorer moorland on a nearby area of Dartmoor might offer the chance to make some money. Perhaps he could improve the land, drag up the rocks, level the ground, clear the trees, drain the bogs ... he could always use chemicals to clear the weeds, add fertilizer to force the crops. He felt sure he could change the land, make it profitable – he'd made a fortune from farming land before. The site he chose was an area called Crockern Tor.

The businessman began to contact local people – he needed men to cut trees, men with digging equipment, strong horses to drag large stones and pull a plough to cut up the soil.

After a few days the man from Manchester was on-site making his plans, when an old man came walking slowly along the lane. Even more slowly, with the help of his hazel stick, the elderly man made his way carefully over the rough ground towards him.

'Sir I must speak to you,' he said. His eyes were a clear, pale blue.

'Yes, what's the problem?'

'I have no problem sir, but I feel that you do. I must tell you something.'

'Right, what's the problem?'

'Sir, the spirit of these old moors is awfully upset with you.'

'What?'

'I have to warn you – you cannot force these moors to serve you.'

The businessman stared into the elderly man's face.

'I'm sorry, I don't understand what you mean,' he said sharply.

'Listen, I had a dream, a special dream, the sort that feels so clear you know you have met with something living. Old Grandfather Crockern came to me – he won't let you continue with your plans here. It's dangerous what you're doing … you must stop, these moors are powerful.'

'This is nonsense!' replied the businessman impatiently.

The old man's gaze became direct, his tone stern. 'I have lived here all my life; these moors are in my bones. I have known Old Crockern all my life, and you do not understand his nature. He has given me a message for you.'

If only to humour the old local, the businessman put down his papers and pen.

'Alright, go on … I will listen, but then I must get on.'

'The spirit of these moors, Old Grandfather Crockern, laid a vision across my mind. I saw you working, I saw you draining bogs and the water come back by morning. I saw you lift rocks and loose hold of them so they roll and smash your carts. I saw you try to plough and the plough blades break on stones in the soils. I saw you try to build barns and storms come to rip down your work. Old Crockern will not let you change his land. He loves these rough old moors. He will strip you of everything you have if you touch the water, or disturb the earth and the birds and the animals. Heed my words, you cannot work against nature – there is power in the Earth which is far bigger than you. If you so much as scratch his grassy, bracken-brown back, dig into his peat heart, Old Crockern will rip out your pockets until you have nothing left, and then nature will return to itself.'

With that the old man turned and left the newcomer standing just where he was. But the businessman didn't believe the old fellow. He shrugged his shoulders, turned away and carried on regardless.

He drained the bogs. They filled up by morning. He tried to lift big stones – they seemed to have a life of their own and rolled away to smash all in their path. Carts and tools had to be replaced, which cost him money. He tried to plough up the rough land to make good fields, but the stones in the soil broke the ploughshare in minutes, which cost him money. After that the horses refused to work. He built a barn but as soon as it was finished a storm blew in and ripped off the roof … which cost him a great deal of money. The developer started to worry. He pushed on but everything he tried to do fell in ruins. He wouldn't give up, but in the end he was broke. Old Crockern watched the man from Manchester pack his bags, and leave.

Within weeks rough grasses covered over the scars made by the cutting plough blades. Small animals quietly returned to mend their trodden-down burrows. Barn Owl moved into the remains of the abandoned, broken barn. Reeds moved into the bogs, new seedling trees began to reach for the light by the lane side. Old Grandfather Crockern returned to his favourite boulders within the heap of Crockern Tor. There he settled.

Old Grandfather Crockern dreamed the moors … the rocks, the rain, the snow, the sun, the storms, the soils, the rivers, the plants, the animals, the birds, the insects, and the people …

And so it is.

7

CUTTY DYER

A Story Inspired by Traditional Devon Folklore

One icy winter night, Cutty Dyer was resting in his favourite spot just beyond the outskirts of Ashburton village. On the bed of the River Ashburn he sat, perfectly in his element, listening. Down in the belly of the river running waters brought news of rain shedding from the moors, voles burrowing, and herons fishing. Cutty watched as ages old stones turned over and over until they became smooth river pebbles. Deep time flowed.

Little was seen of Cutty Dyer by the human folk, since he was a creature of inky shadows and too deep water. Some said he was a water sprite, some said he was an ogre who had taken to hiding in places where the river was dangerous. They said that his heart was as dark as the deepest blue dye. Worried parents warned their children often – don't play too close to the water, Cutty will get you!

On this night all the children were safe in bed. All was quiet, until a loud shout fit to split wood and wake the dead shattered the midnight air. Two human voices were carried bubbling and spitting over the rippling surface of the river. Harsh words bounced rudely off the underside of the bridge where Cutty Dyer liked to rest. The voices came closer – two men were shambling along the riverside. One wore a big old torn coat, the other a big old battered hat. Neither had both. Torn Coat and Battered Hat. They were squabbling bitterly.

Cutty slid out from beneath the purple shadows of the bridge, and rose to the surface of the water. His large head made a darker shape glimmering in the unreliable, cloud-bothered light of a waning moon. He was massive in the water, a great sopping bulk. His hair floated in thick ropes as he opened first one huge, round,

lamp-light shining eye, and then the other, to see what had come to disturb his peace.

On the bank of the river, not six feet away, Battered Hat complained, 'I'm telling you, we're going the wrong way!'

'No! It's this way, you useless bilberry-picker!' Torn Coat yelled, turning his back to the fast flowing, ice-cold river. He took a step backwards and wobbled dangerously, his feet slipping on the muddy bank. He was a fraction away from falling into Cutty's arms.

Ever so slowly, Cutty reached one dripping, weed-tangled hand towards the tail of the old torn coat.

Battered Hat caught sight of two huge gleaming circles in the night – they seemed to hover in the air behind his friend … then a row of gleaming, jagged, triangular teeth … a black shadow looming out from a freezing, too-deep place.

'**Ahhhhhhhhhhh!**' he screamed. 'It's Cutty, it's **CUTTY!**'

'What?'

'**RUN! RUN NOW!**' He grabbed his friend

by the arm and began to drag him away from the riverbank, slipping and sliding in the wet. A rumbling bubbled from under the water, through the riverbank and up into Torn Coat and Battered Hat's struggling bodies. Their staggered senses became submerged with the low roar of the river – the knocking and scraping of rocks, clinging roots and flooding mud, so loud as to drown out all else. The men fled for their lives, in two different directions, squawking like panicking hens.

Peace returned to the riverside. Cutty looked at a strange abandoned thing squashed in the mud of the riverbank, picked it up, tasted it a little on the edges of his sharp, shark teeth ... but it was just an old battered hat. He withdrew slowly, gently back to his favourite place in his world beneath the water. There he settled, in his element, watching, and listening, as deep time flowed.

8

VIXIANA

Tall Crow, Mother Night,
Teach us Vision and Fearless Fight.
Black Hen, Red and White,
Show us Wisdom, Dark and Bright.

Okey was a young man, as sharp as a clear spring morning, with a strong will and a bright skip in his stride. His slight body moved easily, lithe beneath a simple shirt, moss-coloured cotton trousers and long leather coat. He came from the Okehampton area of Devon.

He loved to walk on the moors. A satchel over his shoulder held a rough chunk of loaf and bottle of good ale. He could walk all day, roving his way to the tor tops and exploring the valley depths. He would stand on the land, throw back his head and reach out his arms wide to the buzzard-blown sky. The moorland birds, animals, pixies, and the sheep-worn pathways loved him too, because they knew he stepped lightly on the earth and he was kind. And so the winding tracks blessed him with a safe passage. Red deer, badger, hare, blackbird and sparrow came close and shared their songs and wild stories with him. And one brightening dawn while he was out in the fields, a pixie native had tugged on his sleeve and given him two precious, magical treasures – the gift of being able to see easily through even the thickest moorland fog, and a shining silver ring.

It came to pass one day that a dark cloud passed over Okey's bright world – he caught wind of a foul witch, Vixiana. Two men had been talking amongst the market stalls in Okehampton – Okey listened in. They said the witch was killing people. Lone travellers, those who were unaware of the darker moods of the moor, were being led astray along a difficult stretch of path. They said it was happening by the Vixen Tor, not far from Princetown and Tavistock. The witch was covering the path with an unnatural fog which confused people more than if they were pixie-led. The unwary travellers would lose their bearings, lured by the treacherous hag as she called to them as sweetly as she could manage. The unfortunate souls would stumble into a dead, cold bog at the foot of Vixen Tor, to the witch's hideous delight.

Okey took a long, calm view of the situation – a traveller's path was being terrorised by a witch? Who would dare blight his precious moorland with such horror? He made a decision to investigate the dreadful, ill-wishing creature.

Okey set off the following morning with his satchel packed, his silver ring tucked in his shirt pocket, and a determined set to his jaw. He strode the long miles easily. Perhaps it was the scream of a raven or the yelp of a fox that alerted his attention as he neared Vixen Tor. Okey scanned the skyline – a black tower of granite loomed ahead. A shadow fell over the land and un unnatural cloud rolled along the path towards him. It gathered and settled deliberately over Okey, creeping heavily, green and cold against his skin. But Okey, the keen-eyed hawk, could pierce through the hateful fog with his pixie-blessed vision. A thin figure, silhouetted atop the Tor, was watching him. Ravens flew raggedly overhead.

'I see you, witch!' Okey whispered through gritted teeth – he was not afraid of things which came from the dark. He slipped his silver ring onto his finger and vanished from sight – by the might of pixie magic the ring made him invisible! Vixiana screamed with rage as he disappeared – a wrenching, thin, whistling wail. She spied the tussocks and hillocks with her own sharp eyes for him but, cloaked in magic, Okey crept towards the Tor. He could see the witch perfectly through the crowding, searching mist as he grew closer.

Vixen Tor towered over one hundred feet high – a monumental pile, stone-faced, watching over the moor. It sat on the land like a great lion, an Egyptian sphinx. Some say that once some dark thing had slid its way from the shadows deep below, made its way between the nearby bronze age burial chambers to the foot of the Tor. Some said, perhaps the creature was a goblin awoken by a spell made by Vixiana herself. It had climbed below Vixen Tor, rolled clicking boulders this way and that, chewed the granite and scrapped a wet hole in the mud to make a cave. This was where the witch lived.

Okey made soft, cat-paw strides to the wide base of the Tor, taking care to step alongside the edge of any dangerous bog. Then up he climbed, up past the Raven's nest, and scrambled onto the top of the great rocks. Vixiana was standing there right before his eyes, leaning over the edge of the Tor and pointing into the mist with her twisted stick.

She was a tall crow. So old was she that the local people could only ever remember her being old. Whip-thin beneath her gorse-torn dress, her back bent taut like a hunter's bow. Big kneed she was, skinny ribbed, and wide through the hips. With a cruel grin, two peg teeth jutting, her face twisted with grim intent. Her pin-hole eyes were set so deep it was as if she was looking out from somewhere far away. She was pointing nastily with one bone finger, muttering foul words, her eyes raking the ground for her new victim. Okey positioned himself squarely on level stone behind Vixiana.

'I see you, monstrous Black Hen! Wicked Stick!' cried Okey, still invisible. Vixiana tottered an awkward turn, enraged.

'Who dares to taunt me? Come where I can see you!' cried the witch, seething.

'Fiendish curse! Demented murderer of souls – you will terrorise this place no more!' Okey tore off his ring. Shocked by Okey's sudden appearance, old Vixiana took one fatal step back. Her heel caught nothing but air. And then she was falling … falling backwards, her thin skirts flapping like the wings of the ravens. Vixiana's own toxic fog

wrapped around her as she fell ... down ... down ... down into the bog, into her own cold trap. So, the dark, wet earth took her from this world into the next. Not a ripple was seen, not a sound was heard from her again.

Okey stood very still, just where he was. Raven landed on the rocks near him and looked him in the eye. A quietness settled over the place. Sunshine broke between the clouds and warmed the rocks and the reeds and the swelling slopes of the moors. A little red she-fox came out from between the rocks at the base of Vixen Tor, slipped quietly away over the moor, and never looked back.

9

BOWERMAN THE HUNTER

Once upon a time, a group of women made their way up to an ancient stone circle on the moor. Blunt granite stones encircled the space, and low hawthorns grew all round, wind-twisted and gnarled. The clear-eyed women's long cotton skirts brushed the ground as they walked. A ceremony began – a fire set beneath a black pot, words, herbs and oils added to clear spring water to make a potent brew. They hummed like the bees as they worked. Then all in a circle the women began to sing their sacred spells.

A few miles away Bowerman the Hunter whipped his dogs into line and mounted his already sweating horse. He was an imposing man, tall, dark, and straight-backed. In a certain light perhaps, his beard could look a little blue. His pack was the largest and the finest in the area, and he was in a savage mood for hunting. All day he rode hard with little luck, but late in the day a large hare leaped from the clitters and bolted away. Bowerman spurred his exhausted horse into a furious chase after the wild animal. Full tilt between some low hawthorns they went, leaped over a low rock, and crashed into the centre of a stone circle – women screamed, fell, scattered to hide behind the standing stones. The horse's hard hooves caught a bubbling black pot and sent it crashing over, hot embers were kicked glowing from the little earth pit onto the grass. Bowerman's terrified horse threw its head high, eyes wild as he wheeled around the circle, trampling and smashing herb bundles and wild flowers.

'Stupid witches and your mumbo-jumbo! Get out of my way!' he screamed. The women cowered by the stones, afraid of being trampled by the horse.

'What harm do cause you? Leave us be – or trouble will come this!' cried one of the women.

'I'm not afraid of your nonsense! Silly spells and songs!' growled Bowerman.

'Leave us alone, or your own actions will come to bite you!' yelled another. Her leg was bleeding, caught by the teeth of a confused hound.

'What rubbish!' snarled Bowerman. 'Ridiculous crones! Stay out the way of my dogs lest you end up my quarry!'

'Leave us alone! You have been warned!' the eldest of the woman insisted.

Bowerman snorted in disgust. Cruelly he pulled his horse round by the metal bit in its mouth. In a chaotic flurry of stamping hooves and panting hounds Bowerman left the clearing and rode away over the moor towards his farmstead, leaving the women enraged at the destruction of their sacred work.

In the weeks and months which followed Bowerman and the witches kept an uneasy distance. Bowerman had no respect for the women and their ceremonies. The circle of witches were furious that their arts be treated with such disrespect – Bowerman attacked their reputation, telling everyone they were fake and powerless. After a time the women decided Bowerman the Hunter must run into a hard lesson. They made a plan, knowing that Bowerman's hunt would cross their path on the moor again.

One of the women was a gifted shapeshifter. She could become any animal she wished. At the right time, on the right day, she transformed herself into a red fox, and ran over the moor to just the right place. The other wildish women made their way purposefully up onto the moor. They arranged their pot over a lively fire, added sharp-smelling powders to bubbling spring water. With focused intent they began to chant strange words and sounds, their bodies swaying in time. A cold wind picked up suddenly, carrying the sounds of thundering hooves and baying dogs – Bowerman the Hunter was abroad, tracking quarry over the moor. The women's voices grew louder, chanting. Over the hill came Bowerman, galloping his horse and dogs furiously after a fleeing fox straight towards the circle of women. The fox came streaking into their midst like a red dart. The hunter thundered into their circle, his eyes blazing, his mouth spitting cruel words and hurling them like hard stones at the women. His dogs swarmed around him, howling. The witches held their ground, chanting louder:

Proud Eye, mind of stone!
Dog's Bane, heart of stone!
Stone Face, bones of stone!
Bowerman, man of stone!

Bowerman slid off his horse to his knees on the turf and stared at the witches in horror – something strange was happening. Power pulsed round the circle, Bowerman felt weak, fear took his heart.

'What are you doing?' he screamed. A coldness began to spread from the ground along his legs, as though the Earth were reaching for him. His face had become ashen, as pale and green as the belly of a bream. The witches swayed and raised their arms to the sky. Bowerman became ridged, petrified – as he slowly turned to hard, cold stone.

Like a storm blowing itself out, the maelstrom ceased. Silence descended. The black-coated women opened their eyes. Before them stood a huge granite stack, a pile of rock, barely recognisable as a man – only the rugged

suggestion of his face remained, and a jutting outcrop that was once Bowerman's nose. At the foot of the granite stack every loyal dog lay, a stone boulder for ever more.

10

THE FAIRY OINTMENT

Eye spy with my left eye,
A fairy prince who rides through the night,
Leaping deer and silver leaf,
Find the gold and catch me a thief.

Nurse Morada lived not far from Holne Village. She was a woman with a broad face, short and stoutly built. She wore wide skirts and her hair tied back in a hard little knot. Not a local woman – no one knew where she was originally from, and they never did trust a stranger. People said she liked to sit huddled over her leather purse and count her money – precious silver coins went in, but never came out. Some even said she was a witch. Even so, many people sent for her when they were ill since she was a good nurse and there were very few doctors in the area.

One late summer evening, with harvest time just around the corner, the sun sailed low to the edge of the world and black thunder clouds gathered over the moors. A storm was surging over the moor, galloping in. The first jagged spear of lightening flashed overhead with a crash. Morada was afraid of the storm, even her cottage appeared to huddle to the ground as grey rain arrived to hammer against the windows. The noise was enough to frighten the dead. She crept nervously up creaking wooden stairs, early to bed. But before she could even hope to settle she heard a tremendous banging and clattering at the front of the house.

'What can that be?' muttered Morada, startled.

BANG! BANG! BANG! – somebody hammered at the door. Reluctantly she shuffled out of bed and over to the small window. Lightening cracked overhead, illuminating a dark shape in the garden – the shape of a great black horse. On its back, looking up at Morada, was a tiny man wearing a hat and a cape.

'My wife needs your help! Will you come to her?' the small man shouted.

'In this weather? No, I will not,' yelled Morada, fighting with the window shutters in the wind. The tiny man held out a leather bag.

'Ten gold coins for your trouble?'

Morada stared at him for a moment, then shut the window, dressed quickly and went down to the front door. The man was standing there, holding the reins of his horse. He was astonishingly beautiful – large dark eyes and long dark hair falling in waves from beneath the broad brim of his hat. He wore clothing made of rich red velvet, a collar of silken lace, and a cape finely embellished with embroidered silver leaves. The horse was magnificent; strong and sleek, his bridle studded with gems and the saddle cloth emblazoned with the image of a leaping deer.

'Please come with me ... I will take great care that no harm will come to you,' said the man urgently. When he spoke, his voice trilled with the sounds of a flute playing and a skylark singing. He opened the purse, gold coins glinted brightly within.

'Alright then,' grumbled Morada. Even her fear of the storm and that huge black horse wouldn't keep her from ten pieces of shining gold. She wrapped a thick cloak over her shoulders and pulled her plain felt hat down hard over her ears.

'You must promise never to speak to another soul, alive or dead, of where we go tonight – or it will go badly for you,' said the tiny man. Morada caught the man's stern expression. She nodded quickly in agreement. The horse, his sides shining slick with rain, stood as still as rocks as she climbed up behind the fairy man – such as he must be. Then into blackness she was plunged as a silken scarf was bound round her eyes.

The horse pushed off into the crashing storm. Lost in a heaving sea of howling wind and driving rain and great waves of plunging, bucking galloping strides, Morada hung on for dear life. Yet not once did she slip on the horse's broad back, not one drop of stinging rain found its way through her cape. The fairy man's magic held her safe.

Until, as though they had stepped through a veil in the storm, all became still. The horse steadied to a gentle walk. They arrived clattering over cobbles into a courtyard and halted. Still blindfolded, Morada was guided gently down. With firm ground underfoot, the fairy man led her into his home. She had to stoop low to go through an oaken doorway. Through long corridors they walked – Morada couldn't see the shimmering silver and gold threaded tapestries on the walls. The images wove themselves into ever-shifting pictures of fairy castles, enchanted forests, gryphons and unicorns. She didn't see the twinkling fairy lights which floated in the air before them as they walked.

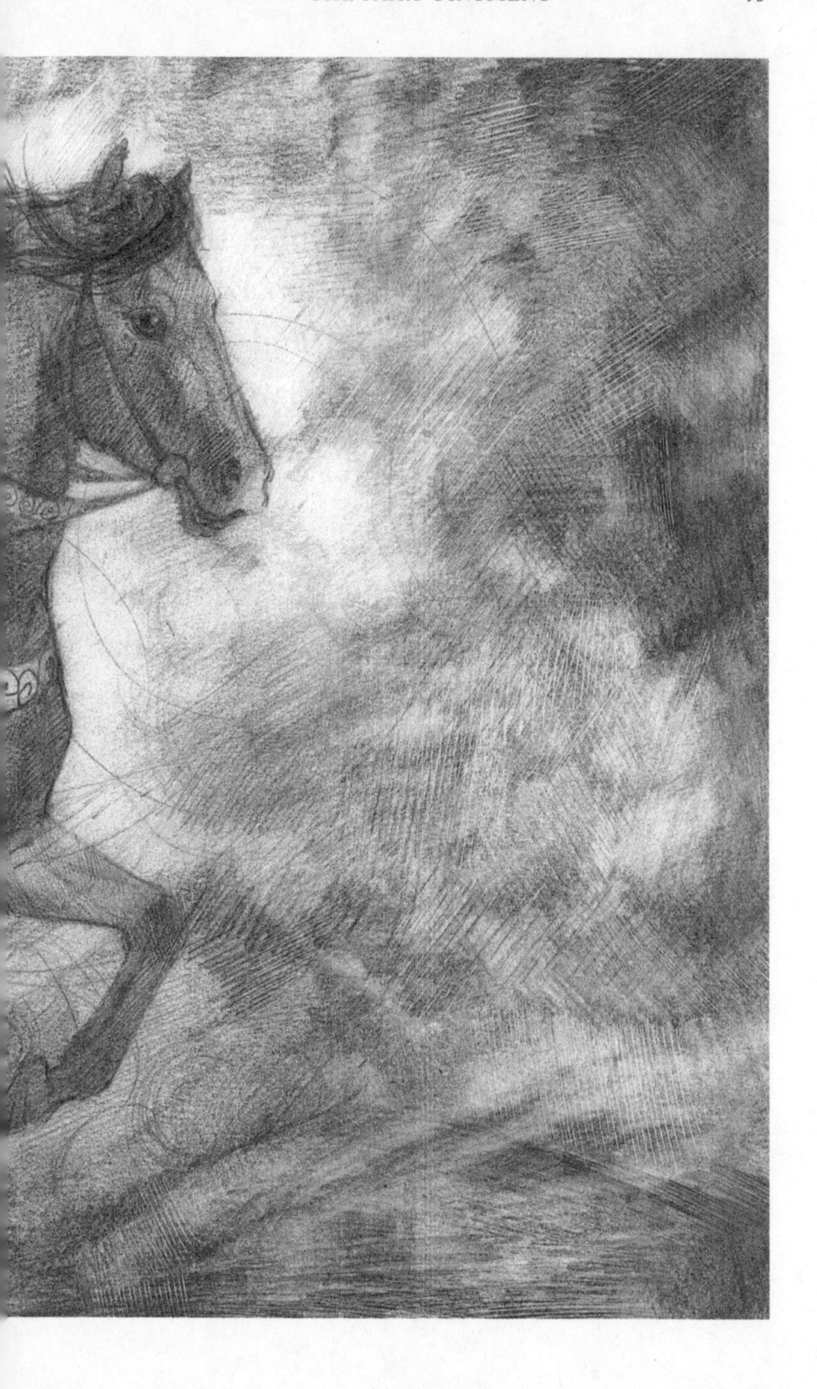

Finally, they arrived into a warm chamber. The silken cloth was removed from Morada's eyes. She blinked against the brightness of a thousand tiny star-lights which sparkled against the dark walls of the room. Before her was a small but luxurious bed, and sitting on the bed holding her belly, a tiny woman. She was an exquisite creature – huge dark eyes, a rosebud mouth, hair falling in silken spirals to her waist. And she was having a baby!

Morada knew just what to do, and she got to work. After a long while which felt like no time at all, a tiny dot of a baby boy was born. He was so small you could have put him in a bun case. A pip of a creature, but strong and healthy.

The fairy man held out a jar of ointment to Morada. A creamy mixture shimmered faintly in the pot – it smelled of geranium and roses, and something strange Morada couldn't place.

'Dab a little of this onto his eyelids,' he said gently. Morada did as she was asked and then without a thought, as she had done a thousand times with a thousand useful things, she popped the jar in her apron pocket. Morada wrapped the little one in a soft little cloth and carefully gave him to his mother.

They sat for a while and the fairy woman told Morada stories of their bejewelled fairy kingdom, and that her husband was in fact a fairy prince, and she a fairy princess. She was given tiny, delicate biscuits to eat and thimble-cups of sweet honey mead to drink. The proud father, the fairy prince, gave her the ten gold coins, and it was time to leave.

With Morada blindfolded again and mounted on the horse, they rode away. The journey home passed in a blur. In no time at all the silken cloth slid from Morada's eyes and she was allowed to drop to the ground outside her own front door.

'Thank you! You have helped us and we are grateful. Remember your promise – not a word to anyone about where you have been and what you have seen tonight, and all will be well.' With that the prince raised a hand as his black horse rocked onto his haunches, half-reared in salute and whirled away, galloping into the night.

Morada ran into her cottage just as the first hints of dawn were showing over the moor. She shut the door firmly behind her and hid her bag of ten gold coins in an earthenware pot by the hearth. Only when Morada climbed wearily back up the stairs to her room, and untied the bow of her apron, did she discover the little pot in her pocket – the fairy ointment! A little shocked to find it there, Morada put it on the shelf for safekeeping.

'No doubt he'll come back for it,' she mumbled to herself, and decided to put the little pot out of her mind. After several days and no sign of the fairy prince Morada couldn't resist temptation any longer.

'Why should I not take a little for myself?' Morada whispered under her breath. 'Magical fairy ointment would be a precious treasure to add to my gold and silver coins. Perhaps I could even sell a little of it for good money at the market?' She decided the fairy prince had most likely not even noticed it was missing.

As the lid came off the jar the air became drenched in the sweetest scent of geraniums and roses, and a strange fragrance Morada couldn't identify. She poked a finger cautiously into the jar. A tiny dab of ointment on the eye couldn't do any harm … could it? Morada patted the cream onto her left eyelid. Nothing happened. Perhaps the gentlest tingling sensation but nothing more.

'So much for that then!' said Morada. She plonked the pot back on the shelf.

The next day Morada woke at the usual time, but when she opened her eyes it was as though she could see two worlds at the same time! Through her right eye she could see the ordinary world, much as it had ever been, but through her left everything was different. This world was extraordinary! The light streaming between the window blinds refracted into rainbow rays, spilling stained-glass pools of colour over the whole room. Her plain knitted blanket seemed to be finely embellished with embroidered designs – plants with curling tendrils, flowers, butterflies. The plain old dresser now appeared ornate, richly carved with oak leaves and acorns. Morada's ordinary clothes, when she stood unsteadily to dress, seemed transformed into the gown of a fairy princess. When she looked out of the window the blackbirds glowed ultraviolet blue, the trees streamed light from their leaves, and even though the day was brightening, she could see all the way to the stars, so piercing was her vision from her left eye.

Morada grabbed the fairy ointment in alarm, stumbled down the stairs, looking only with her right eye, and ran out to prepare her pony and trap.

'I will go to Ashburton to see if I can get something to put this right ... I don't want fairy-sight! What if trouble comes of this?' Morada muttered to herself as she fussed with the pony's harness. She hadn't meant to take the ointment pot, but now she had gone and used the ointment the fairy prince might think she had stolen it!

Morada drove the pony and trap at a hurried trot all the way to Ashburton with only her right eye open. But when she walked into the market street she couldn't resist taking a peek with the left. The street was busy, not only with human traders and local folk – but fairy folk too! There were many of them, fair and richly dressed. And there were pixies, hiding in baskets, scrumping apples and stealing little treasures from the stalls – a silver thimble here, a blue button there – pixies everywhere! The human folk wandered about their business and when Morada looked at them it was as if she could see into their hearts – those whose hearts were full of goodness shone brightly. Those whose thoughts were dark appeared to walk in their own shadow.

As Morada gazed at the scene with her stolen magical vision, the sound of a horse trotting came ringing along the street – a huge black horse, with powerful strides, and the fairy prince riding high!

'You can see me!' the prince said sternly as he arrived alongside. 'You have taken that which does not belong to you. This will not do!'

'I didn't mean too! It was in my apron pocket!' cried Morada. She cowered low, the horse and the prince towering over her.

'But you still chose to take the pot for yourself, even when I gave you ten gold coins – greedy woman! To which eye did you apply the ointment?'

'To my left eye,' sobbed Morada.

'You should not have taken that which does not belong to you and which you do not understand! Give me the pot! You will lose the vision in your left eye and nothing can be done about that.' He reached down from his horse and touched Morada lightly on the left eye. Morada trembled and shook. She had lost her fairy-vision, she had lost the sight in her left eye completely.

'What a shame you took too much … it has cost you dearly,' said the fairy prince. 'Although, my wife was so grateful for your help that I was returning to give you ten more gold pieces for your efforts. Here they are.' He handed Morada a leather purse, heavy with coin. With that the great black horse bowed his head, and away they went, never to be seen again. Morada's sight never returned to her left eye, but she had enough fairy gold to keep her well for the rest of her days.

11

THE WAGGONER'S WISE HORSES

Sweet Breath, Wise Eye,
Ever over moorland roam.
Earthen Bones, horse of mine,
Safely, gently, take me home.

One winter morning, a long time ago, two horses stood together in a stable. Outside it was so cold that spoken words froze in the air, until they thawed in spring and could finally be heard. The horses' warm breaths made dragon-smoke clouds in the dark. They were Devon pack mares with mottled brown, bear-fur thick winter coats, broad backs, deep girths, and mealy-muzzles. Their bones were as strong as oak, as strong as truth. They were gently sharing the last of their hay.

The horses' ears pricked sharply as a sound came from the inn. A man shut the oak door behind him with the click of a latch. Sparkling, iced gravel crunched underfoot as he crossed the yard. He approached the stables, huddled in a shabby coat, hat pulled down hard. Smoke from a peat fire had soaked his clothes, the sharp smell met the sensitive noses of the two waiting horses.

'Time for work my beauties. Early start today,' he said softly. It was four o'clock in the morning, and they had twenty miles to go. The horses breathed warmly over their old handler, checking for bits of apple.

The horses knew their job well. They stood square while the waggoner sorted leather straps and buckles, lifted heavy collars over their heads. In days gone by the tracks and green lanes were too rough and wet for

wheels. Waggons and carts were almost unheard of, the horses had carried heavy cargo on their backs. These powerful Devon pack horses could walk five miles in an hour bearing almost seven hundred pounds loaded onto a crook and crub saddle, safely over the open moor. But today the two horses had a waggon to pull. A heavy load of wood was to be collected from a local estate – ten miles there and ten hard miles back.

At last they were ready. The waggoner led them out of the stable and hitched them to a sturdy waggon, and hauled himself aboard. In his younger days he had walked endless miles along the old herepaths with a team of six tough Dartmoor ponies. They had carried everything you can imagine over the open moor – wool, timber, salt, peat, even household items when needed. Now many of the lanes and tracks were made good enough for the carts to pass through and everything had changed. The old packman worked with his two good, experienced Devon pack mares and was mightily glad of a lift on the waggon.

'Walk on girls, you know your way,' he said gently. He wrapped his legs in a woollen blanket and relaxed back into his seat. The horses pulled away, sure and steady, onto a well-trodden track. They had travelled this way many times and the packman trusted his horses completely. The thud and click of the horses' feet beat out a gentle rhythm while the waggon swayed and creaked. Soon the old man fell asleep, and began to snore. They travelled along in this way for quite some time.

Until the waggon came to a sudden, shuddering, jolting halt.

'What? What is it?' the old man exclaimed, shaken from his sleep. Both horses were rooted to the ground, trembling, staring into a dark patch of woodland ahead.

'What's wrong girls? We've been through here many a time. There's nothing to be afraid of!' Peering into the dark, the man strained to see what was the matter, but nothing appeared on the path ahead. Still, the horses snorted and shook. They refused to move. The waggoner got down from his cart and went to whisper in their ears in the way of the old horsemen.

'There now, gently now … easy girls,' he soothed, trying every way he knew to calm the two mares. But they wouldn't budge. Stock still they stood, staring and trembling. The old waggoner tried apple from his pocket, that didn't work. Half an hour passed – the waggoner began to worry they'd be late home if they didn't get on, so he climbed aboard the waggon and flicked his whip high over the mares' heads – **CRACK!** The horses leaped in the air like they'd been stung by a hornet. Yet they moved forward not an inch.

'I don't like to do this, girls, but we must get on!' said the waggoner, and **CRACK!** He lashed the whip in the air above their heads. The horses shook and still refused. Again the whip snaked out and lashed the air – **CRACK!** The horses took a great lurching leap into their leather collars and were away full tilt. With great galloping strides they pulled the waggon bouncing and swaying a full mile through the woods and even faster out the other side.

'Woah! Woah! Slow down!' The waggoner tried to ease the pace but he was thrown about the waggon seat like a ragdoll. He could do nothing but hang on for dear life until finally the horses slowed to a hard trot, sweat and foam flecking their flanks. On they went like this for another full two miles or so, unheeding of any direction from their driver.

Another half mile down the road and the horses were exhausted. They slowed to a heavy walk, breathing hard, sides heaving. The old waggoner pulled his blanket back onto his knees and untangled the reins, his whole body trembling with fright.

'What on Earth was that about?' he muttered in confusion. He had worked with his team for long enough – never had he seen them be anything but sensible.

The rest of the journey took an age; the horses were so weary. Lanterns were being lit and pot of stew already cooking when they pulled into their destination. The old waggoner settled his horses and went to find himself some supper.

It took a full day to load the timber securely, and the next day the man and his horses set off for home. The waggoner was nervous as they approached the woods – would the horses panic again? Would they bolt? But the two mares walked on calmly, as if nothing had ever happened. It was only when the old waggoner stopped at an inn to water the horses, a rest before the last pull home, he heard gossip.

'Did you know a pack pony train has been robbed? Two days ago in the early morning I'd say,' one jobber from the wool trade said excitedly.

'No! Where? When?' the old waggoner replied, his eyebrows raised.

'It's terrible!' the old guy said. 'Everything stolen, cargo and cash, and even one poor man left for dead! In the woods where the lane runs through – you must have come that way?'

The old waggoner went pale, his hands shook a little.

'In the woods you say? But I went that way with my team and waggon about that time!'

The jobber let out a low whistle.

'Maybe you just missed the robbers – scoundrels could have been there hiding in the woods! I bet the pack pony team arrived not long after you went through there.'

'My horses went crazy, spooked and galloped us through the woods ... I've never seen them do anything like it ... perhaps somehow they knew.'

'Aye, well you were lucky! These routes are dangerous for men like us – murdering thieves all over the moor. We risk our lives for some cargo and coin.' The jobber shook his head bitterly.

The waggoner took leave and returned to where his horses were tethered by a stone water trough. They stood square, patient as ever, as he buckled the harness and hitched the waggon, checked the load. With gentle movements the waggoner went to his horses' heads. They touched him with their whiskered noses, blew gently into his face.

'Ah, my horses, my girls ... thank goodness for your wisdom. I think you may have saved my life,' he whispered with a tear in his eye. With that he climbed aboard the waggon and settled himself with a blanket. Quietly, the man, horses and waggon plodded and rolled along the last lanes home, safe for another day.

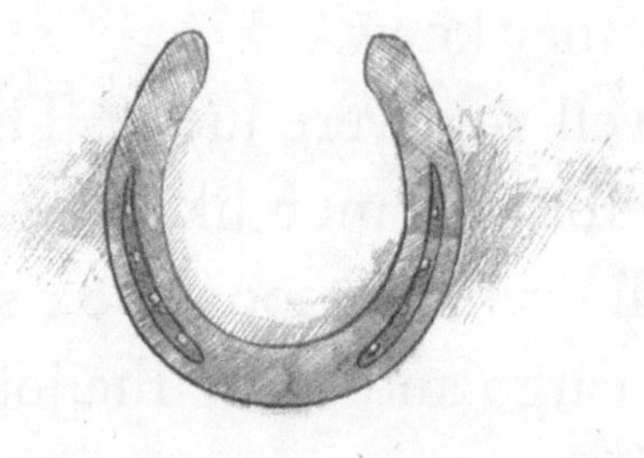

12

THE DRAGON OF O BROOK

A Story Inspired by Traditional Devon Folklore

A dragon awoke slowly from a long, deep dream ... perhaps it took many years for him to first open one glittering golden eye, and then the other. Creatures were stomping noisily on the surface of the Earth above where the dragon lay. He heard heavy boots squelching through bog, tripping over tussock and stone, and the squeak of wooden wheels cutting ruts through peat. Ponies and cattle went over with a thudding beat of all four feet. Sometimes voices shouted rudely over the gentle rush of his beloved waters of the River O Brook. They had disturbed his centuries-long sleep.

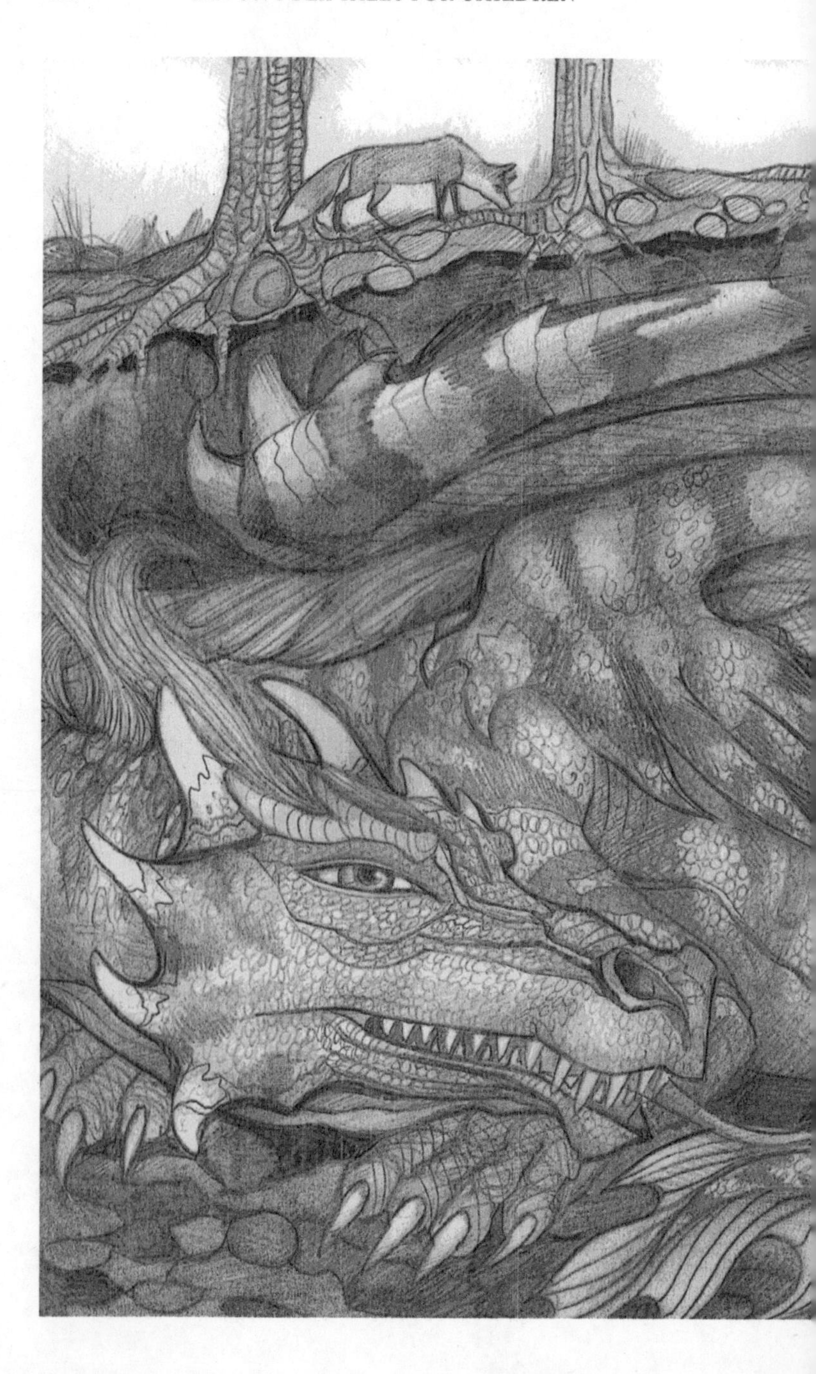

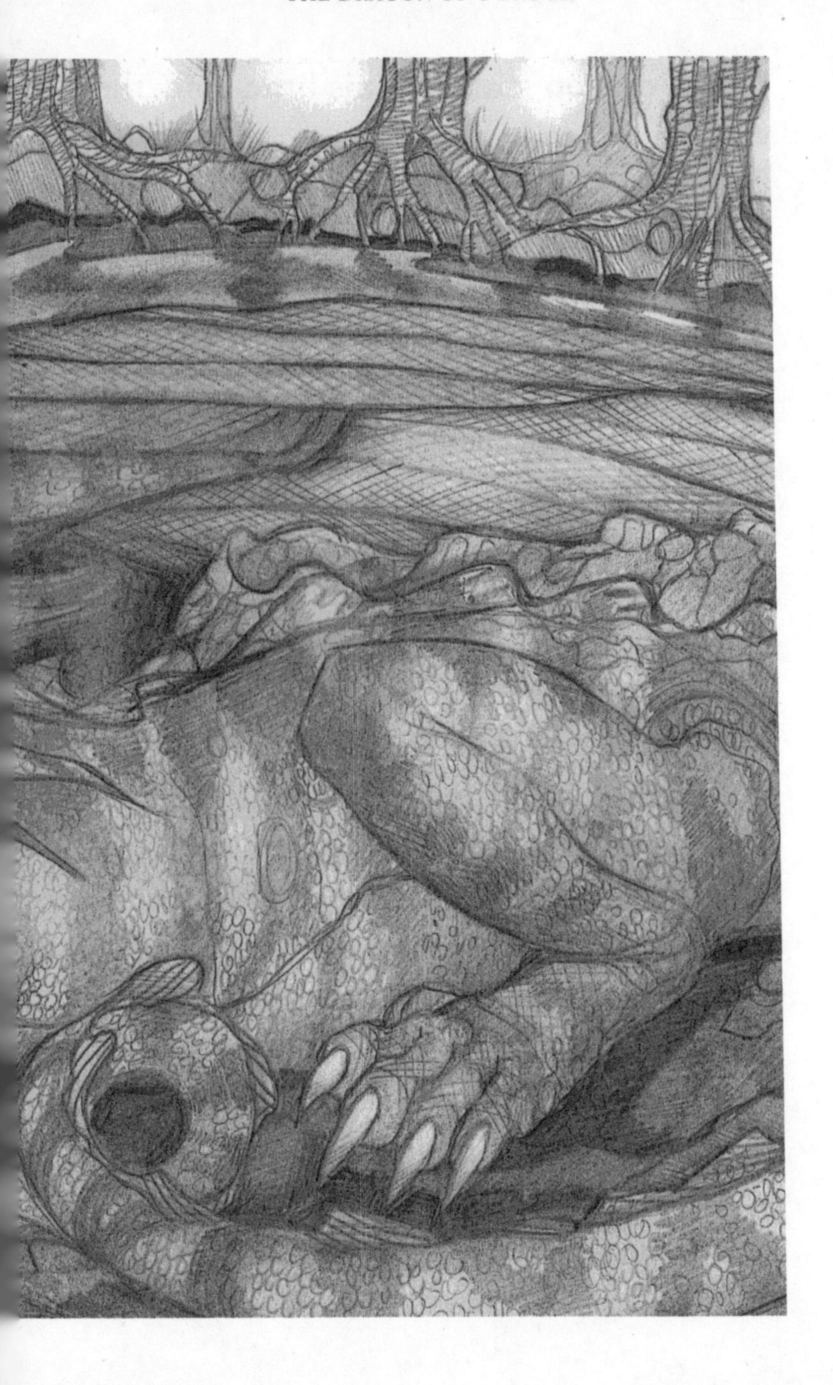

The dragon stretched his lithe body the whole hillside long, his grass-green scales flashing with kingfisher blue, red and gold lights. He yawned, blew out a great, hot, gusting sneeze. He was hungry.

Slowly he lifted himself up to emerge above ground into the twilight of a cool autumn evening, the earth quaking with his movements. Small birds scattered into the safety of brier and bush for the night. Fox witnessed the dragon rising and coiling like a shimmering mist from the Earth. Barn Owl watched the dragon take a long, cool drink from the waters of O Brook. His first for an age. Raven flew up and away with the news, the Dragon of O Brook was awake.

Sheep went missing, and then cattle. Feral ponies began to avoid the area. After a while a traveller who had followed the O Brook, failed to arrive at his destination. Then a whole train of pack ponies and their handlers went missing. People began to huddle in corners whispering … something massive moved like shadow, turned within the shapes of the land, something you couldn't quite see. Bright lights cracked and flickered just above ground. Violent storms blew in, but only over a hill or two, and then vanished in an unnatural way. The toughest moormen from the area crept up near the river to investigate. There they saw a colossal serpent, plain as day, perched on the ancient ruins of a bronze age dwelling. The creature's scales glittered and shone, its claws curved like the blade of a scythe. Like a cat it sat, while its long tail snaked and lashed. Neat rows of dagger teeth glittered in its open jaws, as it surveyed the land for another easy meal. The men crept away terrified.

'It's a dragon! Death to us all!' they whispered down in the village. People hid behind closed doors and drawn curtains.

No one knew what to do. A time came when a knight might ride over the hills and valleys seeking to prove their worth, perhaps win the hand of a fair maiden. But even they refused to fight the dragon. In later times still, nearby tin mines were abandoned. The hills became empty, and silent.

The dragon enjoyed the peace. Eventually he became full. The darkness of his home below ground, with its warm soil-rich smell, called to him, spoke of sleep and dreaming. His golden eyes grew heavy. In his favourite place by the waters of O Brook, he curled and coiled, stretched and settled himself. The great dragon turned slowly over, rolling the mantle of the moors over himself, a thick turf blanket to cover his body. He dropped slowly, deeply into the Earth, yawned, and became still. He slowly closed one glittering golden eye, and then the other. After a century or two of drifting and dreaming, he was asleep.

If you didn't know better, you might have thought there was only a hillside there, by the gentle waters of the River O Brook.

13

JACK O LANTERN

A Story Inspired by Traditional Devon Folklore

One warm August Saturday a young tin miner received word that his brother was ill. Hurriedly he packed his satchel with a chunk of bread, a little cheese and a bottle of water, and having done this, set off to Princetown where his brother lived. It was a quite late in the day and he had some eight miles or so to travel over the moors.

The walking seemed heavy-going from the start. Oppressive weather closed in by the first milestone. Clouds swept over him, making low moves across the sky, cutting the last shreds of evening daylight in half. He trudged on along the heather-edged trackways, over wet slopes, slogged through sopping grass. Drizzle began to obscure the view dangerously. Not even a mile or two further on the dusk half-light rapidly rolled into darkness. The young man stumbled and pitched along. He could no longer see a milestone, a crag, or even the track. In confusion he lurched to a sliding muddy halt. Surely he was halfway there? But then it was the same to go back – no point in that! The ground was getting wetter, the footing treacherous. The young man knew too well the dangers of unseen bogs in the dark. Fear settled on his collar like cold fingers. Shivering, he turned round and round slowly in the dripping blackness, trying to see the way.

He struggled forwards, tripping and tipping over reeds as the ground became ever more saturated. Sodden peat oozed underfoot like black treacle. For hours the lad staggered on with no solid ground to stand on. Bewildered he began casting randomly in all directions, seeking a firm path, but his feet went under. The young man sank to his knees in the bog, his trouble deep. Dread caught him by the heart.

'Oh help! I am lost! I am lost!' he cried to the swirling rain and black moors.

A light flickered in the distance. Could it possibly be? The lad fought against the sucking mud to get to his feet. Breathing hard, he stared into the dark. There again! – a faint glimmer, a blue-green light – a lantern surely? Just when he thought there was no hope – a fellow traveller to help him?

'Help me! Help me!' he cried, and lunged desperately towards the lantern light. But as he drew a little nearer the light danced a little further away. As he slogged through bog he could just make out a flickering greenish-blue light, but never a person there to carry it. He cried out again and again but no answer came. He wondered if he was being pixie-led to nowhere. But follow the light he must, dragging himself through pools of swamping mire. He drew a little closer. There it was – but it was a light all by itself, hovering just three feet above the ground. The lad stared at the little ball of illumination.

'Oh, it's a Jack O lantern!' he whispered in dismay. Not a human soul was there to give him hope.

The little light hovered before him, a wavering flame in the air, a bright spirit dancing in the dark. Some say they are the souls of those forever lost in a dark night, some say they are a living spirit from the earth. Perhaps it would help him find his way to safety, perhaps it would lead him into the dark forever. Who can say what nature will do? The young lad stood up and resolved to go on. He accepted his fate. There was nothing else to do but step forward bravely towards the light.

'Take me where you will,' he said. The little light danced away and he followed. As he drove himself forwards he found a firm tussock, and then another, and another. Heather brushed against his legs, turf pushed back against his aching feet – dry ground! The young man stopped, his hands on his knees, exhausted. He gazed at the little blue-green light. For a few moments it hovered in eerie

silence, a salute in the dark, and then slowly, gently, faded away.

'Thank you,' the lad said. He paused a while, gratitude pouring silently from his heart.

Calmly the young tin miner walked on, new hope beating in his chest. A way had opened before him. And, just as the dawn light reached over the silvered edge of the world, he was greeted by the merrily twinkling lights of Princetown

14

THE TIN MINE GOBLIN

A Story Inspired by Traditional Devon Folklore

The boy crept into the tunnel. Darkness swallowed him in moments. Only the flame from his lantern which he held high before him threw a glow against the narrow tunnel roof and sides. Figures seemed to leap out from the black lines between rocks and dance in the lamplight. He felt with his feet for the metal tracks which ran down the centre of the tunnel. Men had laboriously crawled and burrowed into the rock seeking rich seams of ore – the metal lodes which lay hidden like glittering secrets in the dark. Wooden tubs were filled with rubble and ore by the miners, and pushed along the tracks and out into the streaming daylight.

Stuck through the boy's belt was a small hammer, in his hand a pick, and slung over his shoulder a leather bag. Inside were packed a flask of water and a thick-crusted pasty made by his mother, still slightly warm from the oven, and his six candles. The boy's heart beat hard and fast. This was his first day of work down in the tin mine.

The heat was becoming intense, but he must push on – no work meant no pay. He was thirteen now, grown enough to do more than break up rubble on the surface, and his mother was depending on him. The hammer blows of a work gang carving relentlessly into the rock walls echoed along the tunnel. To his relief he came upon them, blackened and hot, their mouths covered by grimy clothes to keep out the dust. One of the men turned slowly, eying the new boy.

'You look strong enough for a good day's work! Go along that tunnel there. Take this bucket – there's a pile of rubbish needs scooping into a trolley for taking up to the surface.'

'On my own?' asked the boy.

'Yep. Don't worry, it's a strong tunnel, it won't come down on your head,' the man said. The boy didn't feel so sure. He knew all too well the numbers of men lost every year in the mines.

'Watch out for the goblins though.'

The boy froze. He had been trying not to think about them.

'Goblins?'

'Sure, there are goblins here – the Tin Mine Knockers. Keep your wits about you! They may be friendly … or maybe they'll break your tools, snuff out your candle and leave you down there, alone in the dark.'

'If you're really unlucky they'll bring the roof down,' another of the men snapped.

'Leave them a good piece of your pasty so they know you're a friend – perhaps then they'll be good to you,' an older miner suggested earnestly. He coughed and wheezed as he spoke.

The entrance of the tunnel opened wide like a jagged black mouth in the wall. The boy held out his lantern as far in front of him as he could and walked in, stumbling over loose scree. After what seemed like an eternity the sounds of the miners tapping and knocking with their hammers had faded and all he could hear was his own rough breathing and echoing footsteps. Then he arrived at the blunt end of the tunnel. Everywhere was strewn loose rock from fresh mining, left there since it seemed that particular hole had offered the miners only hard graft and no treasure. Two empty wooden trollies stood waiting. The boy lit a fresh candle and used hot, dripping wax to fix it onto a little ledge in the tunnel wall. He began to collect up the stones, their clattering almost unbearably loud in the eerie silence underground. For hours he toiled in the heat and the dust.

After a time, the oddest feeling stole over him, that somehow he was being watched. Faint scratching and scrambling sounds caught his attention. The boy stopped working. *What was that noise all the way down here?* He kept perfectly still, listening.

'*Tap, tap, tap.*'

The small sound echoed into the pocket of space in which the boy crouched. It was as though a small hammer were knocking against the rock … *but on the other side of the wall!*

'*Tap, tap, tap, tap.*' The knocking was louder this time.

Cautiously, the boy crept closer to the rockface. Holding up the lantern, he examined the crevices and cracks, searching for some way through, some clue that there could be sound coming from some work-team close by, or even rats perhaps?

On the other side of the wall, standing on the mother lode of precious tin ore, one of the Little Men, a Tin Mine Knocker, watched the boy through the thin veil of rock. Their faces were inches away from each other. Just for a second the boy thought he caught a glimpse, a split-second impression, of a small, bright-eyed, bearded face looking at him from within the rocks.

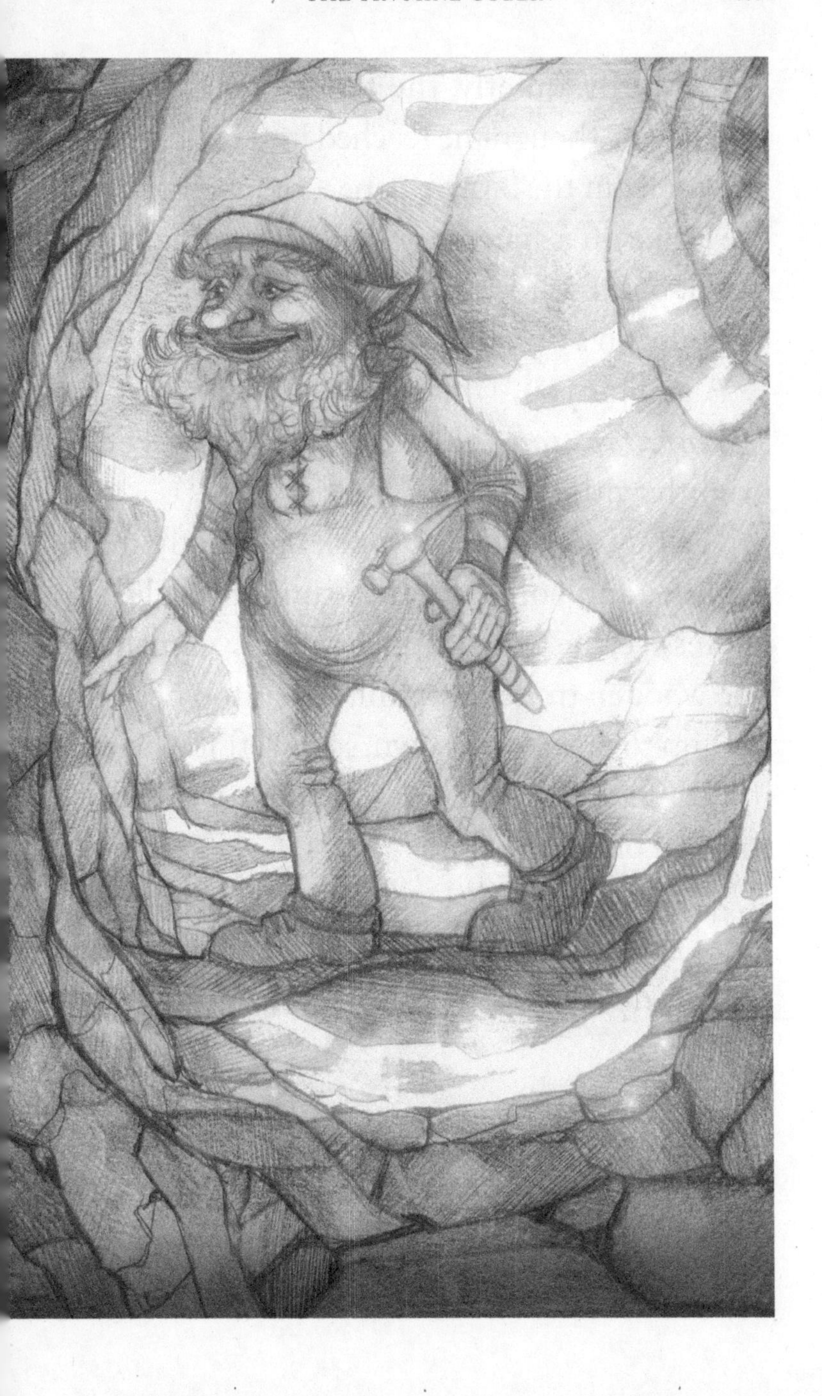

Carefully, quietly, the boy stepped back. After some thought he reached into his satchel and took out the brown-paper-wrapped pasty. He broke off a generous chunk, for a moment held it out towards the wall, and then placed it carefully on a broad stone.

'A gift for you,' whispered the boy.

'*Tap, tap, tap,*' the Knocker answered brightly with his small silver hammer.

The boy continued to work on quietly for a while, and somehow the tunnel felt less oppressive, the work a little lighter. Eventually one wooden trolley was full. It was too heavy for him to push on his own, so he left it where it was. Gathering his tools, he turned to face the wall one more time.

'Perhaps you will lead me to the mother lode? I'll be here again tomorrow.'

'*Tap, tap, tap,*' came the answer.

15

VICKEYTOAD

We-ha-neck! We-ha-neck!
Well aplowed! Well asowed!
We've reaped! And we've a mowed!
Hurrah! Hurrah! Hurrah!

One year, when the golden sun began to ride its great chariot in a low arc across the sky, it was harvest time. Cries of 'Wee yen! Wee yen!' were heard ringing across the fields. Men's voices were laughing and shouting – it's time for 'crying of the neck!'

It was Farmer Fernley's favourite celebration. The day before he had cut his last field of wheat. The wheat was gathered into neat shooks, bundles of golden stalks all neatly tied at the middle, and stood in orderly rows on the stubble. That morning he excitedly caught up his great black and white shire horse in the paddock, took him to the farmyard and harnessed him to the wain. Off they went, the great shire plonking his bucket-feet heavily on grassy track, steadily hauling the wagon to the top field. Farmer Fernley was expecting to see his neat work all waiting for him. On arriving he was astounded to see that all his tidy bundles of wheat were strewn from one side of the field to the other. It was a wild mess. The farmer stared, dumbfounded.

'Who on Earth would want to pull my good work to pieces?' he exclaimed. He frowned hard. None of the locals would do such a thing. Undoing good work was no joke. Could it be the pixies? Farmer Fernley had no problems with the pixies, he had never so much as said a word against them. Yet it had to be the most likely answer.

After a while the farmer could do nought else but rake up all the wheat, bundle and stack the shooks all over again. It took all day. By the time the work was done he could hear the farmers and reapers shouting for the 'crying of the neck'. Rather than be seen to be the last to finish and miss all the fun he left the shooks standing in their rows, jumped up on his wagon, and joined in the procession that was wending its way down the lane.

The reapers gathered together, having a fine time. One expert old fellow, master of the ceremonies, had gone round the shooks and selected the finest ears of wheat he could find. Skilfully he made a perfect bundle, tied at the middle until it looked like a golden doll – the 'neck'. This he raised proudly above his head.

'The neck! The neck! The neck!' he cried. The crowd jumped about laughing and whooping, arms and hats raised in the air.

'Wee yen! Wee yen! Wee yen!' the old fellow cried again. The people jumped about and threw their hats in the air until one of the men grabbed the 'neck' and ran as fast as fury to the farmhouse. Holding a pail of water, a young woman stood ready to block his way and give him a good soaking if he tried to get past. The 'neck' itself was carefully put away, to be kept and ploughed into the first furrow on 'plough Monday', the first Monday after Twelfth Night, as a prayer for abundance and next bountiful harvest.

They crowded into the farmyard next, all the horses were fed, watered, and turned out to stretch and roll away the work of the day. This done the feasting began. Tables were loaded with hams, cheeses, rustic loaves, fruit and flagons of cider. But as the hours stretched on Farmer Fernley had an uneasy feeling in his belly, stuffed though it was with meat and ale – what if his beautiful wheat shooks were somehow wrecked again? Close to midnight he withdrew from the celebrations. Through shards of cloud-broken moonlight he made his way slowly up the grassy lane. He crept along an old stone wall, and leaned, doubled over, to peer through the sheep creep into the top field.

A hundred little pixies, maybe more, were dragging the shooks from where they stood. Gangs of them turned them over. They worked hard to pull the wheat bundles to pieces, laughing all the while. They danced and jumped and stamped on the outrageous mess of stalks. Wheat was strewn as far as it could be thrown by such small creatures, tossed into the air, ripped to bits.

Farmer Fernley stood up square and watched them in plain sight, but they didn't care. Two squat little pixies laughed and danced right in front of him.

'Get off my shooks, you pesky little toad!' yelled Farmer Fernley as he shook his fist at the nearest pixie. The pixie stopped his little jig and pointed at Fernley.

'Ha! Ha! Ha! He doesn't know that's my name! My name is Vickytoad! And it means "little toad"!' cried the grinning, pointy-faced pixie to another.

'Ha! Ha! Ha! You are a "little toad"!' laughed his friend hysterically.

Farmer Fernley stood and stared. He scratched his head. He had no idea what the pixies meant, or why they found such joy in wrecking his wheat.

'I guess you can't always understand the ways of nature,' he said. With that he shrugged, turned, and stomped away back to the farm. He'd have to pick up his shooks again, but that was work for another day.

16

FOX AND THE PIXIES

Back along, in a time when a fox and a pixie might not always get along, an old dog-fox was hunting. Winter was bitter and food had been terribly scarce. He had a smart nick in his tail where a farmer had caught him with a shot from his gun, since he had crept onto the farmyard trying for a fat chicken or three, so desperate was he. His usual menu of small rabbits, field mice, moles and rats had run him thin, so when he ran into a group of pixies on the moors he didn't think twice about it – he jumped to catch them! Rarely would a fox and a pixie interfere with other's business, and anyway a pixie could smell a fox from a half mile away, but this day they had been so preoccupied by their dancing that they didn't see him coming. They scattered frantically in all directions. Fox shot after the nearest pixie and almost had him as he bolted in through the front door of his tiny house – a shelter made with intricately woven willow sticks.

'Let me in!' growled the ravenous fox, scratching at the tiny wooden door.

'No! You can't come in – I've barred the door!' yelled the pixie.

The fox stood up on his hind legs and – CRASH! – he came down hard on the roof of little woven sticks. He dug in his claws and tore the roof apart – the little sticks scattered all over the ground. Down went the pixie, in through the fox's jaws. But he was a small snack for a starving fox.

'I need more!' he growled.

On fox went, nose to the ground, following the scent of another pixie. He arrived at the front door of a second tiny home – a home built of beautifully put together river stones.

'Let me in!' growled the fox, breathing hard against the little front door because he could smell the pixie inside.

'No! You can't come in – I've barred the door!' yelled the angry pixie.

The fox stood up on his hind legs and – CRASH! – he came down hard on the roof of little flat stones. Again he dug in his claws and tore the roof apart. The little house was laid open – down went the pixie, in through the fox's jaws. But even then the fox was still hungry.

'I need more!' growled the fox.

On he went, nose to the ground, until he found a third tiny home. This time the little house was made of leaf-size pieces of iron. The metal was weathered and rusted to rich patterns of red and orange, and soldered together by silvered magic so delicately a jewellery-maker would have been proud of the work. The fox thought of nothing but the wriggling pixie inside.

'Let me in!' he growled, clicking his teeth against the little metal door.

'No! You can't come in – I've barred the door!' yelled the pixie. He was furious.

The fox reared up on his hind legs and – CRASH! – he came down hard on the little iron roof. It didn't move. He dug in his claws and tore at the roof as hard as he could. Not a single soldered shingle came apart.

'Ha!' yelled the pixie.

Fox was angry but he held his temper. He was a cunning old dog. After thinking carefully for a moment, he said: 'Alright, I mean you no harm. I will make amends for frightening you – let's be friends. If you come out I will show you a field full of well-grown turnips to the left of the farmer's barn – you could have some for your supper. I will carry you there so you will be safe from the farmer's wandering dog. Jump onto my nose so you can climb onto my back.'

The pixie thought for a moment.

'Alright, I will come with you, but not till morning. Meet me here one hour before dawn,' he said.

'Very well,' replied the fox, feeling sure he would at least have breakfast.

In the morning the swift little pixie was up, not one hour, but three hours before dawn. He found his way to the farmer's field and returned home loaded with good, round turnips. Fox arrived just in time to see the pixie dragging the last turnip through his tiny front door. Too late he grabbed at the door with his teeth and scratched it furiously with his claws – it was barred again!

'Oh, where have you been?' said the pixie, innocently. 'You are late. Luckily, I managed to find the turnip field without you. But thank you for letting me know where it is.'

Fox kept his cool. He sat down and stared at the little metal home, and thought for a moment.

'Ah well, never mind,' he said. 'I slept a little late. But I have a better idea: tomorrow is the first day of Widecombe Fair – let's go together. There are sure to be all sorts of wonderful treasures there for you – pots, pans and buttons, and all sorts of shiny, sparkly things – and I will carry them home for you.'

'That would be nice,' said the pixie brightly. 'Meet me here two hours before dawn and we will go there together.'

'Very well,' said the fox, certain that he would at least have breakfast the next day, since he wouldn't be late twice.

Barely had the moon crossed over the middle of the night sky when the pixie was up and out on the road to Widecombe. He stole into the fair just as dawn was reaching over the horizon and all the stallholders had put their wares out for the day. The pixie helped himself to treasures here and there – a clock with delicate cogs, a fat-bellied crock pot, and a shiny new pan. He set off home again. But just as he was dragging his loot down a long slope not far from home the old dog-fox came pelting towards him.

'Thought you'd fool me again did you, twisty little trickster!' roared the fox.

The pixie jumped into the fat-bellied pot as quick as a fish can turn, and set it rolling down the hill faster than the fox could run. When the pot stopped he leaped out and ran for his life the rest of the way home. Fox found only the empty, cracked pot at the bottom of the hill – no pixie to be seen.

Fox was utterly vexed to find himself outwitted again. But he was determined to catch the pixie. He took a strong wooden box, with a sturdy lid and heavy lock, and went again to the pixie's home. When he got there he found, to his surprise, the little door unlocked and the pixie asleep – so tired was the pixie from all his early morning trickery, he had forgotten to secure his little house. Fox skilfully hooked a claw behind the little metal door, reached in, grabbed the pixie and shoved him into the wooden box, locking it tight.

'Got you now, you wriggling, pesky pest!' snarled the fox. The pixie yelped and then went quiet. After a moment he said, 'Let me out and I'll tell you a secret.'

'Not a chance,' said the fox.

'It will change your life forever,' whispered the pixie, beginning to weave a spell with the silvery sounds of birdsong in his voice. Curiosity got the better of fox.

'Very well, I'll open the lid a peep, just for a moment.' He opened the lid and put his ear to the gap, so he might hear the pixie's wonderful secret. By way of a spell, since the pixie had tired of games, he leaped out of the box and stuffed the fox straight in.

'YOU CAN'T FOX A TRICKSTER!' the pixie yelled. He shut the box tight with magic and locked it for good measure.

'Now you get out of that one!' And with that the pixie walked away.

17

THE WITCH'S IMP

Many years ago, a farmer and his family lived peacefully. They were kind, hard-working people, and were considerate to their neighbours. The farmer and his wife tended their children and animals patiently. A small herd of russet-coated Devon Ruby cattle were their pride and joy. Far from rich, they had just one strong horse to plough and pull for them, a few hens to lay good eggs. Yet they were content with all they had.

Perhaps because their happiness shone like sunshine from their home, and their children could be heard laughing in the farmyard, they attracted the attention of an envious witch. She was an icicle-eye, throw-a-black-thought-like-a-poison-dart-at-your-heart kind of a witch. A dark shadow walked with her, a black hen lived in her yard. She could hide a wicked curse behind a smile. And cast a dark curse over the farmer and his family she did, just for spite.

The next morning the farmer's wife ran into the kitchen, tears in her eyes.

'The cows, they're all refusing to eat – they've gone thin as needles overnight!' she cried.

'Not possible,' said her husband. 'They're fat and fit enough for a county show!' The farmer kicked his chair back from the table and rushed out so see. He stared in anguish at his prize Devon Ruby cattle – bones jutting like the parts of a broken fence, lustrous russet coats and shining eyes gone dull.

'How can this be? In all my years as a farmer I've never seen the like!' he pulled his hair in horror.

That night the wife stirred hot broth in an iron pot, cut warm bread. The family gathered round the fire for supper and to talk about what had happened during their day. Just as the meal was finished and the wife had taken out her sewing, the farmer caught sight of a creature sitting on a trivet in the far corner of the fireplace. He froze – and stared. Then he nudged his wife in the ribs.

'Pssssssssst! Look there!' he hissed. His wife plainly saw the frightening little imp – she too was staring at the creature. It was the size of a well-fed cat. Poppy-red hair grew from its head and back and the tip of its tail. With piercing eyes and a startling grin, it stared right back at them. As soon as it had the attention of all the family the imp leaped out from the fireplace and bounced round the kitchen shouting and laughing hysterically:

Grab it, smash it, all to bits!
Farmer's wife is having fits!
Rip it, throw it, break the lot!
Farmer's going to lose the plot!

'CATCH IT!' yelled the farmer. The whole family jumped after the imp, crashing into each other and tripping over kitchen chairs.

The wife picked up a wicker basket and tried to drop it over the imp, and the children chased it with a broom and a mop. The farmer tried to grab the creature but it was too quick. The imp crashed one more time round the kitchen, smashing the honeypot and throwing pots and pans, before bolting straight through the closed wooden door to the farmyard outside. Dazed and bewildered, the family stared at all the mess.

The next day the farmer went out to check the sheep, but instead of finding them foraging peacefully they were hurling themselves round the paddock, galloping this way and that way and back again. A streak of red caught the farmer's eye – a fox he thought. But no, the red imp was riding high on the back of a terrified ewe! Furious, the farmer ran for his gun, but by the time he returned the imp had exhausted the sheep, tired of his fun and run away over the moor.

The Devon Ruby cattle looked worse than ever. The hens stopped laying. Even the horse stood with his head drooping to the floor and wouldn't move. The farmer and his wife began to despair. What were they to do?

That night the family sat round the fire nervously peering into dark recesses and shadowed corners. The imp stuck its grinning monkey-face out from under the peat basket. There it sat, staring at the farmer without blinking and laughing to itself, until the farmer could bear it no longer. He lunged at the imp and tried to grab it by the scruff. The poppy-red monster darted between the farmer's legs and ricocheted round the room, bouncing off the walls. The farmer grabbed his gun from where it rested over the mantle but an invisible force held him by the arms while the imp danced before him cackling. Lurching heavily to one side the farmer managed to reach for an iron fire poker. He swiped hard, crashing round the room after the wicked imp in crazy circles, pots and crockery smashing onto the floor. Round the kitchen the imp jumped, flipped and cartwheeled until it dived into a corn sack by the kitchen door. Whump!

Whump! Whump! – the farmer whacked the sack with the poker until the sack split open and corn spilt all over the floor. But the imp darted out unharmed and flew up the stairs. Screaming with glee and whooping as it went the imp trashed every bed, jumping on every one like a trampoline. Night-pots were hurled against the wall, pillows torn open and curtains torn down. Finally, the imp careered down the stairs, ran through the butter, tipped over the milk and vanished through the wall.

The farmer and his wife stared at the ruined rooms in disbelief. Clouds of pillow feathers slowly settled in the bedrooms. Smashed crockery and a pool of spilt milk lay on the kitchen floor.

'What a mess!' the farmer growled. 'Something must be done! I will go to see the old wise one who lives between the village and the woods. Perhaps she will help us.'

'Maybe she will, but be sure to take the white witch something good in exchange for the work,' said his wife.

'Aye, I understand,' replied the farmer.

With that the farmer's wife gathered the few precious eggs they had left, and wrapped a piece of beautiful embroidered cloth she had just made, and gave them to her husband.

A few miles away, just where the edge of the village met the woods, lived an old woman. Some said she was a white witch. She was one who could call the birds out of the sky and sing songs of flowers and honey with the bees. She was known to be able to weave a powerful healing spell, make a potent herbal brew, unbind a curse. It was said a fox sat beneath her chair, a magpie on her shoulder.

The farmer knocked gently on her door, and when she welcomed him in he took off his hat and placed the gifts of eggs and needlework on her kitchen table. The old healer told him this:

'You have been cursed by a black-hearted woman. Take hawthorn branches and build a big fire, as big as you can. Take a bowl carved from ash – both of these trees will help ward away evil witchcraft – take the bowl to your most prized cow, she who is the most poorly. Take a little of her blood into the ash bowl. Place the ash bowl in the centre of the hawthorn. Set it all alight – if the ash bowl is not burned or cracked by midnight break it all to pieces and release the blood to the fire. Hide all the pieces of the ash bowl amongst the embers and ashes of the fire. If you do exactly as I say, the witch's curse will be undone.'

The farmer thanked the wise woman and left. He followed her instructions exactly, heaping the hawthorn high in the centre of the farmyard. He placed an ash bowl in the centre of the fire, containing a little blood from his best Devon Ruby cow. He settled himself by the fire and kept vigil until midnight, and then took care to see that the bowl was broken open and all the pieces hidden in the embers. At dawn he went to wake his wife.

They crept together to the barn. All the cows were eating steadily, they had gained weight as if by magic, their hides shone with new health. The horse leaned over the stable door and whinnied, keen for a day's work. The hens had laid clutches of large speckled brown eggs. The farmer and his wife hugged each other for joy.

That night the farmer and his family gathered by the hearth. A big pot of stew bubbled and popped over the fire. Before they settled the family cautiously peered into shadowed corners and lifted the peat basket, but the poppy-red imp didn't appear, and, in fact, was never seen again.

18

THE GOLDEN MAZE

What happened was …

Elsa had been left alone to manage the farm. Still a young girl, her father had gone to work at the peat cuttings on Dartmoor, so desperate was he to make ends meet. Mother had died when Elsa was very small, so only she remained to keep the animals well and tend the house. But times were tough, so the farmer had no other option but to pack his tools and set off for the peat ties, leaving his young daughter responsible for their home.

Elsa was determined to do well for her father, so she worked hard to keep the farm running. She was glad to have the loyal company of their dog Jess and grateful for all that was good. In their meadow the grass grew long and lush, and was dotted with many wild flowers and herbs. With such good pasture, their one house cow was yielding two full pails of rich milk every day.

One day, after tending to the evening milking, Elsa and Jess were making their way back to the farmhouse. So careful was she not to spill a drop of the precious milk that Elsa didn't notice three pixies walking along the path towards her. That is, until Jess stopped in her tracks with a low warning 'Woof!' and a hard stare. Elsa watched the three small pixies in astonishment. Beautiful they were – three pixie friends all wearing matching leaf-green jackets and little red hats, chattering and laughing together. Elsa didn't feel at all alarmed by them, she had never given them cause for offence, she was sure.

'Who are you?' the first pixie asked. The sounds of a robin singing and a grasshopper chirping seemed threaded through his voice.

'Elsa,' she answered simply.

'Where are you going?' asked the second pixie. As he spoke it was as though tiny silver bells were tinkling in the air about him.

'Home to make fresh butter with my milk, so I may have some to sell at Tavistock market tomorrow.'

'Ho! You have lovely, creamy milk in your pail – will you give us some?' asked the third pixie, his eyes twinkling as though they gave out starlight.

Elsa gazed at the magical three. They were so small she didn't imagine they could take very much milk, and she naturally liked to share.

'Of course! Take all you can drink,' she said.

One by one the pixies took a turn to drink from the pail. To Elsa's amazement they drank the bucket dry. The third pixie handed her the empty pail, noticing her anxious expression.

'Yes, it is all gone. You will have no butter to take to market tomorrow. But do not worry. Trust that we will repay you for your kindness – in the morning go and look for treasure in your garden!' With that the three pixies vanished in a blink.

Elsa was most distressed by the loss of her milk. Still she could do nothing but hope the pixies would be true to their word and bring her some fortune in return for her generosity. She and Jess went home and settled for the night.

In the morning Elsa went immediately to the garden. The plot by the house she knew was a nest of nettles, ragwort, thistles and docks – a neglected mess, since she had no time or strength left after working the farm to make the garden neat and pretty. Today, she was astonished by the scene which flourished there. Red roses, yellow roses, white roses, pink … a profusion, an abundance, a bounty of beautiful roses bloomed from vigorous, healthy bushes. The flowers which greeted Elsa wrapped her in a thick blanket of rose-scented heaven.

'Oh, the pixies have kept their promise!' she cried. She sat for a while gazing at her good fortune, trying to take in the wealth. Then she set to, carefully clipping and bundling the precious flowers and placing them into the pack-pony's wicker paniers.

In Tavistock the local people were celebrating the feast of St Rumon, and when they saw Elsa's beautiful roses they flocked to buy them to decorate their church. Soon every single rose was sold and Elsa had a little pocket of shining silver coins. She had never seen such a rich day! Elsa's father was coming home for the weekend and she had made a great deal of money to give him.

The weekend arrived and Elsa cooked herself and her father a nourishing mutton-meat stew. She told her story of the three pixies and gave her father the silver coins. Elsa's father stared at the treasure in disbelief – more money than could be made on ten market days normally. He was overcome with relief. With tears in his eyes he insisted that every day they must put out a jug of their best creamy milk, to show their gratitude to the pixies for the gift with which they had been blessed.

Every day Elsa was sure to put the jug of milk on the doorstep for the pixies. The following morning the jug was always empty, and the very next market day Elsa went outside and saw to her delight that they were blessed with a garden glowing with rose blossoms. Off to market she went and sold every one – another pocket of shining silver to give to her father. However, her success did not go unnoticed. The girl on the next stall along, Syntha, had been watching. Even though her father was wealthy, she was envious of Elsa's true beauty, and of her radiant roses. Syntha was the kind of person who was pretty to look at but the ugliness of her thoughts could show at the edges of her expression.

'What beautiful, sweet smelling roses! How have you grown so many? You must be a wonder in the garden – tell me your secret,' Syntha said with a sly smile.

Elsa was an honest and trusting girl so she answered directly.

'We are blessed to have the help of three magical pixies,' she said innocently, and told her whole story about the jug of best milk on the doorstep and their wondrous garden. Syntha took care to look as though she had only a casual interest, but she squirreled away every detail of the information – where Elsa had met the pixies and that it was milk they liked. She decided she would like to profit from the pixies' blessings. After she had shut up her stall she scurried away home, picked up a half-full pail of thin milk left over from the morning, and less the cream which had already been skimmed. Not the best by any means, but Syntha thought it should do. She rushed to the place where Elsa had said she first met the pixies. Sure enough, before long, the three pixies came walking along the lane. No chattering and singing this time, the pixies arrived with solemn faces and their hands stuffed in their leaf-green jacket pockets. They stopped and stared at Syntha in silence. It was clear to them that she had two faces – the one she showed and the one she kept hidden away. Syntha stomped up close to the little people.

'Hello! Goodness, you must be thirsty! Let me offer you a cool drink of milk from my pail.' She plonked the bucket down in front of them.

The pixies eyed her suspiciously. The first pixie took the half-empty pail and looked at the thin milk inside. He sniffed it, and then handed it the second pixie who did the same. The third pixie took the pail and dropped it on the floor in front of Syntha with a clank. With that all three vanished. Syntha was left standing alone, staring at an empty patch of grass and a pool of spilt milk.

Still, Syntha had no clue why the pixies wouldn't like her gift and the next morning she rushed outside to see what they might have brought her. No luxurious tangle of abundance was there to meet her, no glorious display of flowers – instead the garden reeked of rotting vegetation. Brambles trailed over the fence, thorns tore at her stockings. She climbed about in the heap of dead twigs and mess, furious to have not been rewarded for her generosity. Why should she be worth less than a peasant girl like Elsa?

The next market day Elsa's stall was brimming with roses again. Syntha seethed with rage. Later that day she packed up her stall and walked to the Abbey to find the Abbot, determined to bring an end to Elsa's success.

'She is a witch I tell you. The flowers she sells are unnatural, cursed even! You must stop this evil in our midst, send your monks to undo her spells,' she hissed at the Abbot. Syntha had a rich father who had given large gifts of money to the Abbey, so the Abbot felt he must agree. A posse of monks was sent to Elsa's home, much to her surprise. They made a ceremony with bells, a heavy book, and white candles to banish the pixie magic from the garden. Roses withered from the touch of their 'holy water'. The monks left the garden blasted and bare, and Elsa sobbing at the destruction. Never again would wondrous pixie roses grow in her garden.

Still, good-hearted Elsa continued to put a pitcher of creamy milk out for the pixies – it was no fault of theirs that the roses had been destroyed. When the pixies came on the eve of the next market day and saw what had happened to their beautiful rose garden they set to work, refusing to be defeated and see their good-hearted friend go without when she gave always her best to them. They held hands and danced in a circle over the blighted soil, made a pixie ring with their spell-singing. Their robin song, cricket-chirruping, river-bubbling, breeze-whispering voices wove a magic so deep no priest in all the region could make it undone, while the full moon shone blue light upon all that happened.

In the morning Elsa woke, went downstairs, out the wooden kitchen door, and slowly to the garden. Wide-eyed, she approached a new scene which unfolded before her – carrots, radishes, onions, cabbages, leeks, beans climbing high into the air, peas with full pods too, a wild profusion of food packed into every corner of lovingly tended soil. Elsa was stunned by the wealth. Slowly, silently, with her head bent in gratitude, she began to carefully harvest the gifts of the garden into her baskets.

Later, Elsa's father was home again, and she told him about what the monks had done to the rose garden, and how the pixies had woven magic anew. Elsa's father was an experienced man who had seen a lot of life.

'Elsa, did you tell anyone about the pixies?' he asked gently.

'Only Syntha at the market ... she asked me how I could have such beautiful roses. But she is always friendly.'

'You are true and kind Elsa, but not everyone is like you. There are those you meet along the way who may smile and seem welcoming, but on the inside they hide dark thoughts.' Elsa looked at her father in dismay, but in her heart she knew he was right.

A few days later Syntha was on her way home when the three pixies appeared before her. Sytha was shocked, but quickly recognised their leaf-green coats and little red hats. Such was her pride she guessed the pixies had seen their error and come to reward her as they ought. But the trickster pixies had a different thought – this girl was responsible for the ruin of their rose garden.

'Pretty girl, we have come to honour you with our gifts, since you shared your fine milk with us,' said the first pixie as he gave low bow. Syntha was so full of herself that she failed to see the glint in his eye.

'Ask for any reward and we will bring it to you,' said the second pixie, with a wide, toothy grin. Syntha threw her hands in the air in excitement. Impulsively, with eyes lit up with greed, she pointed at one of her father's huge fields. It covered the whole side of the hill.

'Fill this field with gold for me!' she demanded.

'That we will do,' said the third pixie, and tipped his hat. He looked at her with the intensity of a hawk with a mouse in its sights, but Syntha didn't notice. And in a blink the pixies were gone. All that remained were the echoes of their wicked laughter.

The next day Syntha was up before the first rays of daylight reached over the horizon. Holding her fine cotton skirts up to her knees she ran to the field on the hill. The whole area glowed with gold from edge to edge, because it was ram-packed with prickly gorse covered in golden yellow flowers. Syntha screamed in rage.

'This is Elsa's fault! I shall have her seized and taken away, the little witch!' she wailed.

The three pixies were watching, and as they heard Syntha's threats they called together a golden fog. Wisps of mist rose from the ground and wrapped around her, pulled and pushed her as it grew thick and dense. She staggered amongst the gorse, crying and casting this way and that. The pixies led her in deeper, along a path between the bushes. Syntha came to a dead end. She tried another way, it led to three more paths. High walls of thick gorse lined every pathway, they scratched and tore her clothes and pushed her back if she tried to force her way through. Syntha became hopelessly lost in a golden maze she herself had caused to be made.

People wondered and whispered about what might have happened, but Syntha

was never seen at the market again. Yet life continued peacefully for Elsa. Every day she placed a jug of thick creamy milk on the doorstep for the pixies. Each market day she was greeted with an abundance of food bursting with colour and vitality in the garden. Often, in the evenings as the moon began to shine her silver light into Elsa's magical garden, she would sit and listen to the birds chattering in the branches of apple trees outside her open window, and the distant cry of the fox as she walked over the meadow. Sometimes she would hear three pixies singing as they worked their magic into the night, of all that is blessed and true, gentle and wise.

Soul garden, apple trees,
Walk with grace, and love the bees.
Earth treasure, and moonlight spells,
In our dreams the roses dwell.

19

FLIGHT OF THE IMAGINATION

Buzzard soars high in a wild sky above the bracken-bronzed hills of Exmoor. His wings are broad enough and he is powerful enough to carry us home. Below him mealy-nosed, toad-eyed Exmoor ponies are running together over Brendon Common, as wild ponies have done in Britain for thousands of years. They are the old ones who know how to live in harmony with the land. Inland from Exmoor, rolling miles of mid-Devon farmland make rich story-ground for pixies and imps who love to play in the shooks and the hay.

Buzzard

Fly High, See Far,
Lend a broad feather, Air Star.
Wild Cry, Voice Sharp,
Carry us here, to where we are.

In the distance Dartmoor rises like the back of a whale. Through the story-mists Goemagog is walking home over the moor to his family – a Trojan ship blessed by Diana has not yet sailed over the horizon. A train of Dartmoor pack ponies faithfully walk the old routes still, their crooks and packs honouring the old ways. And still a wild hare can be seen running up on the moors – who can say whether she may be a magical shapeshifter who by day lives an ordinary human life.

Across to North Devon we go, following the line drawn by a seam of black coal which runs all the way to the North Devon coast. Ancient forests fell and were pressed into the ground in the Palaeozoic Carboniferous age some 350 million years ago, and were then moved by continental shifts over a vast expanse of time. Now the stories of those ancient trees whisper within the clay called Bideford Black.

From the clifftops we look out to a wild and foaming sea. Once upon a time Cruel Coppinger and bands of murderous pirates ransacked the cargo-laden ships which came to grief against the rugged rocks of this wild coastline near Lundy Island, Hartland, Martinhoe, and beyond. Perhaps the spirits of pirates and smugglers walk the streets of Bideford still.

Away Fox goes into the mists of mythic time. She knows the way to go – a sharp-eyed hunter with a keen ear for a new story, leaving her neat tracks through the dew-wet fields of the imagination. Follow her footprints through Fairy Cross towards to the village of Black Dog – old place names are clues and signposts along the way to a treasure trove of stories. Silvered words weave a silken web above, below, through and beyond every part of the land. Our lives are stitched and sewn together by the stories we share. In the garden, beneath your feet, by the hedgerow, in the street … stories are everywhere. Perhaps if all the stars are in just the right place, and you leave a rich gift on your doorstep, a magical being will sing in your garden. Perhaps even the moon and the whispering trees and the dragon in the hill will come to meet you, and if you tell your story, they will listen.

BIBLIOGRAPHY

BOOKS:

Dacre, Michael, *Devonshire Folk Tales*. The History Press, 2010

Coxhead, J.R.W, *The Devil in Devon: An Anthology of Folk Tales*. West Country Hardbacks, 1967

Sharman, V. Day, *Folktales of Devon*. Nelson, 1952

Whitlock, Ralph, *The Folklore of Devon*. Batsford, 1977

ONLINE RESOURCES:

www.bbc.co.uk/nature/history_of_the_earth

www.sacred-texts.com. Extract: Corineus and Gogmagog by John Milton.

www.legendarydartmoor.co.uk

www.visitdartmoor.co.uk

www.dartmoor.gov.uk - Dartmoor Legends.

www.folkrealmstudies.weebly.com

ADDITIONAL READING

Dinnis, Rob, and Stringer, Chris, *Britain: One Million Years of the Human Story*, The Natural History Museum, 2014

Bray, Mrs Anna, *A Peep at the Pixies: Pixie tales from Ancient Dartmoor by Anon E. Mouse*, Kindle Edition

Green, Christina, *Devon Yarns.* Countryside Books, 1995

Toghill, Peter, *The Geology of Britain.* The Crowood Press Ltd, 2002

SPECIAL THANKS TO:

Sam Goodwin of 'The Dartmoor Pack Ponies' for supplying information about the Devon pack ponies and horses, and the old pack routes over Dartmoor, and supplying the article 'The Devon General Purpose Horse' from the Devon and Exeter Daily Gazette, 18 March, 1887.

Pete Ward of 'EARTH South West' for supplying information about Bideford Black clay and the geology of North Devon.

Since 1993, The Society for Storytelling has championed the ancient art of oral storytelling and its long and honourable history – not just as entertainment, but also in education, health, and inspiring and changing lives. Storytellers, enthusiasts and academics support and are supported by this registered charity to ensure the art is nurtured and developed throughout the UK.

Many activities of the Society are available to all, such as locating storytellers on the Society website, taking part in our annual National Storytelling Week at the start of every February, purchasing our quarterly magazine Storylines, or attending our Annual Gathering – a chance to revel in engaging performances, inspiring workshops, and the company of like-minded people.

You can also become a member of the Society to support the work we do. In return, you receive free access to Storylines, discounted tickets to the Annual Gathering and other storytelling events, the opportunity to join our mentorship scheme for new storytellers, and more. Among our great deals for members is a 30% discount off titles from The History Press.

For more information, including how to join, please visit

www.sfs.org.uk